Free Video   Free Video

Essential Test Tips Video from Trivium Test Prep

Dear Customer,

Thank you for purchasing from Trivium Test Prep! We're honored to help you prepare for your PSB RNSAE exam.

To show our appreciation, we're offering a **FREE *PSB RNSAE Essential Test Tips* Video by Trivium Test Prep.*** Our video includes 35 test preparation strategies that will make you successful on the PSB RNSAE. All we ask is that you email us your feedback and describe your experience with our product. Amazing, awful, or just so-so: we want to hear what you have to say!

To receive your **FREE *PSB RNSAE Essential Test Tips* Video**, please email us at 5star@ triviumtestprep.com. Include "Free 5 Star" in the subject line and the following information in your email:

1. The title of the product you purchased.
2. Your rating from 1 – 5 (with 5 being the best).
3. Your feedback about the product, including how our materials helped you meet your goals and ways in which we can improve our products.
4. Your full name and shipping address so we can send your **FREE *PSB RNSAE Essential Test Tips* Video**.

If you have any questions or concerns please feel free to contact us directly at 5star@ triviumtestprep.com.

Thank you!

- Trivium Test Prep Team

*To get access to the free video please email us at 5star@triviumtestprep.com, and please follow the instructions above.

D1211131

PSB REGISTERED NURSING EXAM STUDY GUIDE 2020-2021

PSB RN Exam Prep Book and Practice Test Questions for the PSB RNSAE Exam

TABLE OF CONTENTS

ONLINE RESOURCES

To help you fully prepare for your Registered Nursing School Aptitude Examination (RNSAE), Ascencia includes online resources with the purchase of this study guide.

PRACTICE TEST

In addition to the practice test included in this book, we also offer an online exam. Since many exams today are computer based, getting to practice your test-taking skills on the computer is a great way to prepare.

FLASH CARDS

A convenient supplement to this study guide, Ascencia's flash cards enable you to review important terms easily on your computer or smartphone.

CHEAT SHEETS

Review the core skills you need to master the exam with easy-to-read Cheat Sheets.

FROM STRESS TO SUCCESS

Watch "From Stress to Success," a brief but insightful YouTube video that offers the tips, tricks, and secrets experts use to score higher on the exam.

REVIEWS

Leave a review, send us helpful feedback, or sign up for Ascencia promotions—including free books!

Access these materials at:

http://ascenciatestprep.om/psb-rnsae-online-resources

INTRODUCTION

The Registered Nursing School Aptitude Examination (RNSAE) was developed by the Psychological Services Bureau (PSB) for use by professional nursing programs during the application process. The exam evaluates candidates' relevant knowledge and skills so that they can be accurately placed in nursing education programs.

What's on the RNSAE?

The RNSAE is a multiple-choice test that includes concepts covered in high school–level English, math, and science classes. The exam will also test your ability to identify relationships between shapes and includes a short vocational test designed to measure your personal suitability to work in health care.

Test	Concepts	Number of Questions	Time
Part I: Academic Aptitude	**Verbal Subtest**: identifying related vocabulary words	75	40 minutes
	Arithmetic Subtest: performing arithmetic calculations		
	Nonverbal Subtest: identifying patterns in shapes		
Part II: Spelling Test	identifying misspelled words	45	15 minutes
Part III: Reading Comprehension	answering questions about the content of short passages	35	35 minutes
Part IV: Information in the Natural Sciences	answering questions about biology, chemistry, physics, and health	60	25 minutes
Part V: Vocational Adjustment Index	choosing to agree or disagree with statements about your personality and workplace behaviors	90	15 minutes

Test	Concepts	Number of Questions	Time
Total		305 questions	2 hours and 10 minutes

Note: Number of questions and time may vary.

How is the RNSAE Administered?

The RNSAE is administered by individual health care education programs. Most programs will require that you take the test at a specified testing location, usually on their campus. You should check with the program to which you are applying to find their testing dates and locations. If you want to report your RNSAE score to a school at which you did not test, you will need to contact the school's admissions office.

Before you take the RNSAE, carefully check the policies and procedures for your particular test site. Fees and payment methods will vary by school. In addition, most schools will have specific requirements for what you will need to bring (e.g., identification, pencils) and what not to bring (e.g., calculators, cell phones).

The PSB allows you to re-take the RNSAE. However, each school will have its own policy about which scores they will accept. Keep in mind that schools may require that you take the RNSAE the same year that you are applying.

How is the RNSAE Scored?

You will receive a raw score and a percentile rank for each of the five tests and three subtests. The raw score will simply show how many questions you answered correctly. The percentile rank will show how you scored compared to other candidates. For example, if you are in the seventy-fifth percentile for the Reading Comprehension test, that means you scored higher than 75 percent of all test takers. If you test at the health care education program to which you are applying, they will be sent a copy of your results.

There is no set "passing" score for the RNSAE. Each program will have its own guidelines for how it interprets your scores during the application review process. Contact your school's admissions office if you would like to learn more about how they use RNSAE score reports.

Ascencia Test Prep

With health care fields such as nursing, pharmacy, emergency care, and physical therapy becoming the fastest-growing industries in the United States, individuals looking to enter the health care industry or rise in their field need high-quality, reliable resources. Ascencia Test

Prep's study guides and test preparation materials are developed by credentialed industry professionals with years of experience in their respective fields. Ascencia recognizes that health care professionals nurture bodies and spirits, and save lives. Ascencia Test Prep's mission is to help health care workers grow.

ONE: WORD KNOWLEDGE

The thirty verbal questions on the Academic Aptitude test will gauge your knowledge of common vocabulary words. You will see a list of five words labeled *a* through *e*, and your job is to find the word that doesn't fit with the others.

> **Verbal Question Format**
>
> *Which word is most different in meaning from the other words?*
>
> **1.**   a. kind b. gracious c. friendly d. vicious e. considerate

Fortunately, to answer these questions, you don't have to know the exact definition of all the words. Usually you'll just need to pick out the word that doesn't match in tone. Having a large vocabulary will obviously help with these questions, but you can also use root words and affixes to determine the meaning of unfamiliar words.

Word Structure

An unfamiliar word itself can provide clues about its meaning. Most words consist of discrete pieces that determine their meaning; these pieces include word roots, prefixes, and suffixes.

Word roots are the bases from which many words take their form and meaning. The most common word roots are Greek and Latin, and a broad knowledge of these roots can make it much easier to determine the meaning of words.

Table 1.1. Common Word Roots

Root	Meaning	Examples
alter	other	alternate
ambi	both	ambidextrous
ami, amic	love	amiable
amphi	both ends, all sides	amphibian

Table 1.1. Common Word Roots (continued)

Root	Meaning	Examples
aqua	water	aqueduct
aud	to hear	audience
auto	self	autobiography
bell	war	belligerent
bene	good	benevolent
bio	life	biology
ced	yield, go	secede
chron	time	chronological
circum	around	circumference
contra, counter	against	contradict
crypt	hidden	cryptic
curr, curs, cours	to run	precursory
dict	to say	dictator
dyna	power	dynamic
dys	bad, hard, unlucky	dysfunctional
equ	equal, even	equanimity
fort	strength	fortitude
fract	to break	fracture
grad, gress	step	progression
graph	writing	graphic
hetero	different	heterogeneous
homo	same	homogenous
hypo	below, beneath	hypothermia
ject	throw	projection
logy	study of	biology
luc	light	elucidate
mal	bad	malevolent
meta, met	behind, between	metacognition
mis, miso	hate	misanthrope
morph	form, shape	morphology
mort	death	mortal
multi	many	multiple
path	feeling, disease	apathy

Root	Meaning	Examples
phil	love	philanthropist
port	carry	transportation
pseudo	false	pseudonym
psycho	soul, spirit	psychic
rupt	to break	disruption
sect, sec	to cut	section
sequ, secu	follow	consecutive
soph	wisdom, knowledge	philosophy
tele	far off	telephone
terr	earth	terrestrial
therm	heat	thermal
vent, vene	to come	convene

Prefixes

In addition to understanding the base of a word, it's helpful to know common affixes that change the meaning of words and demonstrate their relationships to other words. **Prefixes** are added to the beginning of words and frequently change their meaning (sometimes even to the opposite meaning).

Table 1.2. Common Prefixes

Prefix	Meaning	Examples
a, an	without, not	anachronism
ab, abs, a	apart, away from	abnormal
ad	toward	adhere
ante	before	anterior
anti	against	antipathy
bi	two	binary
circum	around	circumnavigate
di	two, double	diatomic
dia	across, through	dialectic
dis	not, apart	disenfranchise
ego	I, self	egomaniac
epi	upon, over	epigram, epiphyte
ex	out	extraneous

Table 1.2. Common Prefixes (continued)

Prefix	Meaning	Examples
ideo	idea	ideology
in, im	not	immoral
inter	between	interstellar
locus	place	locality
macro	large	macrophage
micro	small	micron
mono	one, single	monocle
poly	many	polygamy
pre	before	prescient
sym	with	symbiosis
un	not	unsafe

Suffixes

Suffixes are added to the end of words, and like prefixes they modify the meaning of the word root. Suffixes also serve an important grammatical function and can change a part of speech or indicate if a word is plural or related to a plural.

Table 1.3. Common Suffixes

Suffix	Meaning	Examples
able, ible	able, capable	visible
age	act of, state of, result of	wreckage
an, ian	native of, relating to	vegetarian
ance, ancy	action, process, state	defiance
ary, ery, ory	relating to, quality, place	aviary
cian	possessing a specific skill or art	physician
cule, ling	very small	sapling
cy	action, function	normalcy
dom	quality, realm	wisdom
ee	one who receives the action	nominee
en	made of, to make	silken
ence, ency	action, state of, quality	urgency
er, or	one who, that which	professor

Suffix	Meaning	Examples
escent	in the process of	adolescent
esis, osis	action, process, condition	neurosis
fic	making, causing	specific
ful	full of	frightful
hood	order, condition, quality	adulthood
ice	condition, state, quality	malice
ile	relating to, suited for, capable of	juvenile
ine	nature of	feminine
ion, sion, tion	act, result, state of	contagion
ish	origin, nature, resembling	impish
ism	system, manner, condition, characteristic	capitalism
ist	one who, that which	artist
ite	nature of, quality of, mineral product	graphite
ity, ty	state of, quality	captivity
ive	causing, making	exhaustive
ment	act of, state of, result	containment
some	like, apt, tending to	gruesome
tude	state of, condition of	aptitude
ure	state of, act, process, rank	rupture
y	inclined to, tend to	faulty

Medical Terminology

Below is a list of common medical terms that may appear on the verbal or spelling sections of the test.

abate: become less in amount or intensity

abduction: the movement of a limb away from the body's midline

abbreviate: to shorten or abridge

abrasion: an area of the skin damaged by scraping or wearing away

absorb: to take in

abstain: refrain; choose to avoid or not participate

access: means of approach or admission

accountable: liable or responsible

acoustic: related to sound or hearing

acuity: sharpness of vision or hearing; mental quickness

adhere: hold closely to an idea or course; be devoted

adverse: harmful to one's interests; unfortunate

amalgam: a mixture or blend

ambulatory: able to walk

analgesic: a drug that relieves pain

anomaly: something unusual

aphasia: impairment in ability to speak, write, and understand others

apnea: temporary cessation of breathing

aseptic: free from bacteria and other pathogens

attenuate: to weaken

audible: loud enough to be heard

benevolent: showing sympathy, understanding, and generosity

benign: not harmful; not malignant

bias: an unfair preference or dislike

bilateral: having two sides

bradycardia: slow heart rate

bradypnea: slow respiration rate

cannula: a thin tube inserted into the body to collect or drain fluid

cardiac: pertaining to the heart

cease: stop doing an action, discontinue

cephalic: relating to the head

chronic: persistent or recurring over a long time period

co-morbidity: two disorders that occur at the same time

cohort: a group of people who are treated as a group

collaborate: work together on a common project

collateral: adjoining or accompanying

compassion: awareness and sympathy for the experiences and suffering of others

complication: something intricate, involved, or aggravating

comply: acquiesce to another's wish, command, etc.

compression: pressing together

compromise: an accommodation in which both sides make concessions

concave: with an outline or surface curved inward

concise: brief and compact

conditional: dependent on something else being done

consistency: state of being congruous; conforming to regular patterns, habits, principles, etc.

constrict: cause to shrink, cramp, crush

contingent: depending on something not certain; conditional

contraindication: discouragement of the use of a treatment

copious: abundant and plentiful

culture: the growth of microorganisms in an artificial environment

cyanosis: blueish skin

defecate: have a bowel movement

deleterious: harmful or deadly to living things

depress: weaken; sadden

depth: deepness; distance measured downward, inward, or backward

dermal: relating to skin

deter: to prevent or discourage

deteriorating: growing worse; reducing in worth; impairing

diagnosis: analysis of a present condition

dilate: expand; make larger

diligent: persistent and hardworking

dilute: weaken by a mixture of water or other liquid; reduce in strength

discrete: separate; discontinuous

dysphagia: difficulty swallowing

dyspnea: difficulty breathing

dysuria: difficult or painful urination

ecchymosis: bruising

edema: swelling caused by excess fluid

elevate: raise; lift up

empathy: understanding of another's feelings

endogenous: something produced within the body

enervating: causing debilitation or weakness

enhance: to improve; to increase clarity

enteral: relating to the small intestine

ephemeral: lasting only for a short period of time

epistaxis: bleeding from the nose

erythema: redness of the skin

exacerbate: make more bitter, angry, or violent; irritate or aggravate

excess: the state of being more or too much; a surplus or remainder

exogenous: something produced outside the body

expand: increase in extent, bulk, or amount; spread or stretch out; unfold

exposure: the state of being exposed or open to external environments

extenuating: diminish the seriousness of something

external: located outside of something and/or apart from something

fatal: causing death or ruin

fatigue: weariness from physical or mental exertion

febrile: related to fever

flaccid: soft; flabby

flushed: suffused with color; washed out with a copious flow of water

focal: centered in one area

gaping: to be open; to have a break in continuity

gastric: relating to the stomach

hematologic: dealing with the blood

hepatic: relating to the living

hydration: the act of meeting body fluid demands

hygiene: the science that deals with the preservation of health

hypertension: high blood pressure

hypotension: low blood pressure

imminent: very likely to happen

impaired: made worse, damaged, or weakened

incidence: frequency or range of occurrence; extent of effects

incompatible: unable to be or work together

infection: tainted with germs or disease

inflamed: condition in which the body is inflicted with heat, swelling, and redness

ingest: take into the body for digestion

initiate: set going; begin; originate

innocuous: harmless

intact: remaining uninjured, unimpaired, whole, or complete

internal: situated within something; enclosed; inside

intuitive: to know by instinct alone

invasive: being intrusive or encroaching upon

ischemia: restricted blood flow to tissue

jaundice: yellowing of the skin or sclera

jerk: a quick, sudden movement

labile: unstable

laceration: a rough tear; an affliction

languid: tired and slow

latent: hidden; dormant; undeveloped

lethargic: not wanting to move; sluggish

longevity: having a long life

malady: a disease or disorder

malaise: a general feeling of illness or discomfort

malignant: harmful

manifestation: a demonstration or display

musculoskeletal: pertaining to muscles and the skeleton

neurologic: dealing with the nervous system

neurovascular: pertaining to the nervous system and blood vessels

nexus: a connection or series of connections

novice: a beginner; inexperienced

nutrient: something affording nutrition

obverse: the opposite

occluded: shut in or out; closed; absorbed

occult: hidden

oral: spoken, not written; pertaining to the mouth

ossify: to harden

overt: plain to the view; open

palliate: to lessen symptoms without treating the underlying cause

pallor: pale appearance

paroxysmal: having to do with a spasm or violent outburst

pathogenic: causing disease

pathology: the science of the nature and origin of disease

posterior: located in the back or rear

potent: wielding power; strong; effective

pragmatic: concerned with practical matters and results

precaution: an act done in advance to ensure safety or benefit; prudent foresight

predispose: give a tendency or inclination to; dispose in advance

preexisting: already in place; already occurring

primary: first; earliest; most important

priority: right of precedence; order of importance

prognosis: a forecast

prudent: careful and sensible; using good judgment

rationale: rational basis for something; justification

recur: appear again; return

renal: pertaining to the kidneys

regress: to return to a former state

resect: to remove or cut out

resilient: quick to recover

respiration: breathing

restrict: attach limitations to; restrain

retain: hold or keep in possession, use, or practice

shunt: a tube that diverts the path of a fluid in the body

soporific: a drug that induces sleep

status: relative standing; position; condition

pallor: pale appearance

sublingual: beneath the tongue

subtle: understated, not obvious

succumb: to stop resisting

superficial: shallow in character and attitude; only concerned with things on the surface

superfluous: more than is needed, desired, or necessary

supplement: an addition to something substantially completed; to add to

suppress: restrain; abolish; repress

symmetric: similar proportion in the size or shape of something

symptom: a sign or indication of a problem or disease

syncope: temporary loss of consciousness

syndrome: a set of symptoms that characterize a certain disease or condition

systemic: affecting the whole body

tachycardia: fast heart rate

tachypnea: fast respiratory rate

therapeutic: pertaining to the curing of disease; having remedial effect

transdermal: passing through the skin

transient: lasting for only a short time or duration

transmission: the act or result of sending something along or onward to a recipient or destination

trauma: a bodily injury or mental shock

triage: the act of sorting or categorizing conditions and diseases in preparation for treatment

unilateral: relating to only one side

vascular: pertaining to bodily ducts that convey fluid

vertigo: sensation of dizziness and loss of balance

virus: an agent of infection

vital: pertaining to life; alive; essential to existence or well-being

void: empty; evacuate

volume: the amount of space occupied by a substance

Test Your Knowledge

Which word is most different in meaning from the other words?

1.	a. malice	b. hatred	c. animosity	d. hostility	e. sympathy
2.	a. condense	b. augment	c. boost	d. enlarge	e. expand
3.	a. serene	b. peaceful	c. agitated	d. tranquil	e. quiet
4.	a. bellow	b. shout	c. howl	d. whimper	e. shriek
5.	a. cease	b. persist	c. continue	d. remain	e. endure
6.	a. flourish	b. prosper	c. thrive	d. shrivel	e. multiply
7.	a. obscured	b. apparent	c. evident	d. clear	e. obvious
8.	a. sparse	b. plentiful	c. scant	d. meager	e. thin
9.	a. concur	b. agree	c. oppose	d. approve	e. unite
10.	a. deadly	b. benign	c. lethal	d. fatal	e. harmful

ANSWER KEY

1. e.

Sympathy means "feeling pity or understanding for somebody"; the other four words describe negative emotions.

2. a.

Condense means to "make smaller or more compact," and the other four words mean to make larger.

3. c.

Agitated means disturbed or upset, and the other four words describe the feeling of being calm.

4. d.

Whimper means to "make a low whining sound," and the other four words describe making loud sounds.

5. a.

Cease means stop, and the other four words mean to keep going.

6. d.

Shrivel means shrink, and the other four words mean to become larger or better.

7. a.

Obscured means "to be hidden," and the other four words describe things that can be easily seen.

8. b.

Plentiful means "present in large amounts," and the other four words describe a small supply.

9. c.

Oppose means "go against," and the other four words mean to agree or go along with.

10. b.

Benign means "harmless," and the other four words describe something dangerous.

TWO: ARITHMETIC

The twenty arithmetic questions will require you to read word problems and perform calculations to find the answer. You will not be able to use a calculator.

Arithmetic Question Format

1. A nurse has 25 patients to see in a day. If she has seen 13 patients, how many patients still need to be seen?

    a. 7 b. 8 c. 12 d. 13 e. 38

Mathematical Operations

The four basic arithmetic operations are addition, subtraction, multiplication, and division.

- ✦ **Add** to combine two quantities (6 + 5 = 11).
- ✦ **Subtract** to find the difference of two quantities (10 − 3 = 7).
- ✦ **Multiply** to add a quantity multiple times (4 × 3 = 12).
- ✦ **Divide** to find out how many times one quantity goes into another (10 ÷ 2 = 5).

On the exam, operations questions will often be word problems. These problems will contain **clue words** that help you determine which operation to use.

Table 2.1. Operations Word Problems

Operation	Clue Words	Example
Addition	sum, together, (in) total, all, in addition, increased, give	Leslie has 3 pencils. If her teacher **gives** her 2 pencils, how many does she now have **in total**? 3 + 2 = 5 pencils
Subtraction	minus, less than, take away, decreased, difference, How many left?, How many more/less?	Sean has 12 cookies. His sister **takes** 2 cookies. **How many** cookies does Sean have **left**? 12 − 2 = 10 cookies

Table 2.1. Operations Word Problems (continued)

Operation	Clue Words	Example
Multiplication	product, times, of, each/every, groups of, twice	A hospital department has 10 patient rooms. If **each** room holds 2 patients, how many patients can stay in the department? 10 × 2 = 20 patients
Division	divided, per, each/every, distributed, average, How many for each?, How many groups?	A teacher has 150 stickers to **distribute** to her class of 25 students. If each student gets the same number of stickers, **how many** stickers will **each** student get? 150 ÷ 25 = 6 stickers

PRACTICE QUESTIONS

1. A case of powder-free nitrile gloves contains 10 boxes. Each box contains 150 gloves. How many gloves are in the case?

Answer:

Multiply the number of boxes by the number of gloves in each box to find the total number of gloves.

10 × 150 = **1500 gloves**

2. A taxi company charges $5 for the first mile traveled, then $1 for each additional mile. What is the cost of a 10-mile taxi ride?

Answer:

The first mile will cost $5, and the additional 9 miles will cost $1 each.

cost = $5 + (9)($1) = **$14**

Operations with Positive and Negative Numbers

Positive numbers are greater than zero, and **negative numbers** are less than zero. Use the rules in Table 2.2 to determine the sign of the answer when performing operations with positive and negative numbers.

 Subtracting a negative number is the same as adding a positive number: 5 − (−10) = 5 + (+10) = 5 + 10 = 15

Table 2.2. Operations with Positive and Negative Numbers

Addition and Subtraction	Multiplication and Division
positive + positive = positive 4 + 5 = 9	positive × positive = positive 5 × 3 = 15
negative + negative = negative −4 + −5 = −9 → −4 − 5 = −9	negative × negative = positive −6 × −5 = 30
negative + positive = sign of the larger number −15 + 9 = −6	negative × positive = negative −5 × 4 = −20

A **number line** shows numbers increasing from left to right (usually with zero in the middle). When adding positive and negative numbers, a number line can be used to find the sign of the answer. When adding a positive number, count to the right; when adding a negative number, count to the left. Note that adding a negative value is the same as subtracting.

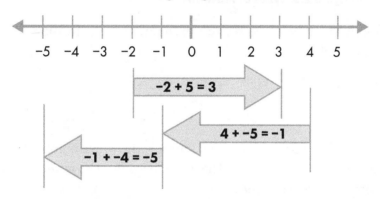

Figure 2.1. Adding Positive and Negative Numbers

PRACTICE QUESTION

3. The wind chill on a cold day in January was −3°F. When the sun went down, the temperature fell 5 degrees. What was the temperature after the sun went down?

<u>Answer:</u>

Because the temperature went down, add a negative number.

−3 + −5 = **−8°F**

Fractions

A **fraction** represents parts of a whole. The top number of a fraction, called the **numerator**, indicates how many equal-sized parts are present. The bottom number of a fraction, called the **denominator**, indicates how many equal-sized parts make a whole.

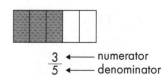

$$\frac{3}{5} \;\begin{array}{l}\longleftarrow \text{numerator}\\ \longleftarrow \text{denominator}\end{array}$$

Figure 2.2. Parts of Fractions

Fractions have several forms:

✦ **proper fraction**: the numerator is less than the denominator

✦ **improper fraction**: the numerator is greater than or equal to the denominator

✦ **mixed number**: the combination of a whole number and a fraction

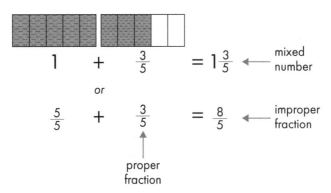

Figure 2.3. Types of Fractions

Improper fractions can be converted to mixed numbers by dividing. In fact, the fraction bar is also a division symbol.

$$\frac{14}{3} = 14 \div 3 = 4 \text{ (with 2 left over)}$$

$$\frac{14}{3} = 4\frac{2}{3}$$

To convert a mixed number to a fraction, multiply the whole number by the denominator of the fraction, and add the numerator. The result becomes the numerator of the improper fraction; the denominator remains the same.

$$5\frac{2}{3} = \frac{(5 \times 3) + 2}{3} = \frac{17}{3}$$

To **multiply fractions**, multiply numerators and multiply denominators. Reduce the product to lowest terms. To **divide fractions**, multiply the dividend (the first fraction) by the reciprocal of the divisor (the fraction that follows the division symbol).

When multiplying and dividing mixed numbers, the mixed numbers must be converted to improper fractions.

 The reciprocal of a fraction is just the fraction with the top and bottom numbers switched.

Adding or subtracting fractions requires a common denominator. To find a **common denominator**, multiply the denominators of the fractions. Then, to add the fractions, add the numerators and keep the denominator the same.

PRACTICE QUESTIONS

4. $7\frac{1}{2} \times 1\frac{5}{6} =$

<u>Answer:</u>

Convert the mixed numbers to improper fractions.

$$7\frac{1}{2} = \frac{7 \times 2 + 1}{2} = \frac{15}{2}$$

$$1\frac{5}{6} = \frac{1 \times 6 + 5}{6} = \frac{11}{6}$$

Multiply the numerators, multiply the denominators, and reduce.

$$\frac{15}{2} \times \frac{11}{6} = \frac{165}{12} = \frac{165 \div 3}{12 \div 3} = \mathbf{\frac{55}{4}}$$

5. Ari and Teagan each ordered a pizza. Ari has $\frac{1}{4}$ of his pizza left, and Teagan has $\frac{1}{3}$ of her pizza left. How much total pizza do they now have?

<u>Answer:</u>

The common denominator is 4 × 3 = 12.

Convert each fraction to the common denominator.

$$\frac{1}{4}\left(\frac{3}{3}\right) = \frac{3}{12}$$

$$\frac{1}{3}\left(\frac{4}{4}\right) = \frac{4}{12}$$

Add the numerators and keep the denominator the same.

$$\frac{3}{12} + \frac{4}{12} = \frac{7}{12}$$

Together, they have $\mathbf{\frac{7}{12}}$ **of a pizza**.

Decimals

In the base-10 system, each digit (the numeric symbols 0 – 9) in a number is worth ten times as much as the number to the right of it. For example, in the number 321 each digit has a different value based on its location: 321 = 300 + 20 + 1. The value of each place is called **place value**.

Table 2.3. Place Value Chart

1,000,000	100,000	10,000	1,000	100	10	1		$\frac{1}{10}$	$\frac{1}{100}$
10^6	10^5	10^4	10^3	10^2	10^1	10^0	.	10^{-1}	10^{-2}
millions	hundred thousands	ten thousands	thousands	hundreds	tens	ones	decimal	tenths	hundredths

To **add decimal numbers**, line up digits with the same place value. This can be accomplished by writing the numbers vertically and lining up the decimal points. Add zeros as needed so that all the numbers have the same number of decimal places.

To **subtract decimal numbers**, follow the same procedure: write the numbers vertically, lining up the decimal points and adding zeros as necessary.

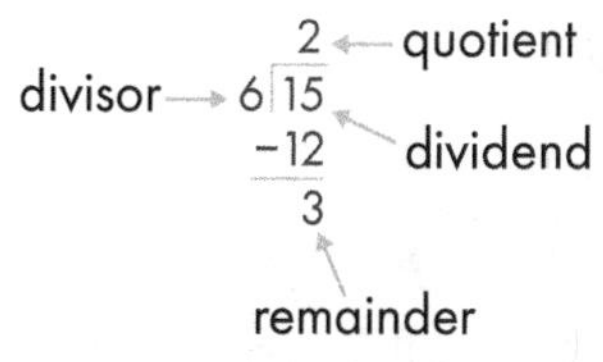

Figure 2.4. Division Terms

It is not necessary to line up decimal points to multiply decimal numbers. Simply multiply the numbers, ignoring the decimal point. Then, add together the total number of decimal places in the factors. The product should have the same number of decimal places as this total.

To **divide decimal numbers**, write the problem in long division format. Move the decimal point in the divisor all the way to the right, so that the divisor is a whole number. Move the decimal point in the dividend the same number of places. Position the decimal point in the quotient directly above its new place in the dividend. Then divide, ignoring the decimal point. If necessary, add zeros to the dividend until there is no remainder.

PRACTICE QUESTIONS

6. A customer at a restaurant ordered a drink that cost $2.20, a meal that cost $32.54, and a dessert that cost $4. How much was the total bill?

Answer:

Rewrite the numbers vertically, lining up the decimal point.

   2.20
  32.54
 + 4.00
  38.74

The meal cost **$38.74**.

7. 1.324 ÷ 0.05 =

Answer:

The decimal point in the divisor needs to be moved two places to the right, so move it two places to the right in the divisor as well. Then position the decimal point in the quotient.

```
          26.48
    005 | 132.40
        - 10
          32
        - 30
          24
        - 20
          40
        - 40
           0
```

8. A carnival ride rotates 2.15 times per minute. If a rider is on the ride for 3.5 minutes, how many times did the rider rotate?

Answer:

This is a multiplication problem.

2.15 × 3.5 =

First, multiply the factors, ignoring the decimal point.

215 × 35 = 7525

The factors have a total of three decimal places, so the answer is **7.525 rotations**.

Converting Fractions and Decimals

To convert a decimal number to a fraction, write the digits in the numerator and write the place value of the final digit in the denominator. Reduce to lowest terms, if necessary.

To convert a fraction to a decimal, divide the numerator by the denominator.

PRACTICE QUESTIONS

9.   Convert 0.096 to a fraction.

<u>Answer:</u>

The final digit is in the thousandths place, so 0.096 is $\frac{96}{1000}$.

Simplify the fraction by dividing the numerator and the denominator by their greatest common factor.

$$\frac{96 \div 8}{1000 \div 8} = \frac{12}{125}$$

10.   Convert $\frac{5}{8}$ to a decimal.

<u>Answer:</u>

$$
\begin{array}{r}
\textbf{0.625} \\
8\overline{)5.000} \\
\underline{-48} \\
20 \\
\underline{-16} \\
40 \\
\underline{-40} \\
0
\end{array}
$$

Ratios

A **ratio** is a comparison of two quantities. For example, if a class consists of fifteen women and ten men, the ratio of women to men is 15 to 10. This ratio can also be written as 15:10 or $\frac{15}{10}$. Ratios, like fractions, can be reduced by dividing by common factors.

11. A company employs 30 people, 12 of whom are men. What is the ratio of women to men working at the company?

<u>Answer:</u>

Find the number of women working at the company.

30 − 12 = 18 women

Write the ratio as the number of women over the number of men working at the company.

$$\frac{\text{number of women}}{\text{number of men}} = \frac{18}{12}$$

Reduce the ratio.

$$\frac{18 \div 6}{12 \div 6} = \frac{3}{2}$$

The ratio of women to men is $\frac{3}{2}$ or **3:2**.

Proportions

A **proportion** is a statement that two ratios are equal. For example, proportion $\frac{5}{10} = \frac{7}{14}$ is true because both ratios are equal to $\frac{1}{2}$.

The cross product is found by multiplying the top of one fraction by the bottom of the other (*across* the equal sign).

Cross product: $\frac{a}{b} = \frac{c}{d} \rightarrow ad = bc$

Proportions have a useful quality: their cross products are equal.

$$\frac{5}{10} = \frac{7}{14}$$

$$5(14) = 7(10)$$

$$70 = 70$$

The fact that the cross products of proportions are equal can be used to solve proportions in which one of the values is missing. Use x to stand in for the missing variable, then cross multiply and solve.

PRACTICE QUESTION

12. The dosage for a particular medication is proportional to the weight of the patient. If the dosage for a patient weighing 60 kg is 90 mg, what is the dosage for a patient weighing 80 kg?

<u>Answer:</u>

Write a proportion using x for the missing value.

$$\frac{60 \text{ kg}}{90 \text{ mg}} = \frac{80 \text{ kg}}{x \text{ mg}}$$

Cross multiply.

$60(x) = 80(90)$

$60x = 7200$

Divide by 60.

$x = 120$

The proper dosage is **120 mg**.

Percents

A **percent** (or percentage) means *per hundred* and is expressed with the percent symbol, %. For example, 54% means 54 out of every 100. Percents are turned into decimals by moving the decimal point two places to the left, so 54% = 0.54. Percentages can be solved by setting up a proportion:

$$\frac{\text{part}}{\text{whole}} = \frac{\%}{100}$$

PRACTICE QUESTION

13. On one day, a radiology clinic had 80% of patients come in for their scheduled appointments. If they saw 16 patients, how many scheduled appointments did the clinic have that week?

    Answer:

    Set up a proportion and solve.

    $$\frac{\text{part}}{\text{whole}} = \frac{\%}{100}$$

    $$\frac{16}{x} = \frac{80}{100}$$

    $16(100) = 80(x)$

    $x = 20$

    There were **20 scheduled appointments** that day.

Estimation and Rounding

Estimation is the process of rounding numbers before performing operations in order to make those operations easier. Estimation can be used when an exact answer is not necessary or to check work.

To round a number, first identify the digit in the specified place. Then look at the digit one place to the right. If that digit is 4 or less, keep the digit in the specified place the same. If that digit is 5 or more, add 1 to the digit in the specified place. All the digits to the right of the specified place become zeros.

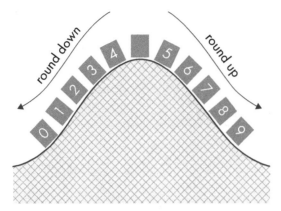

Figure 2.5. Rounding

PRACTICE QUESTION

14. In September, Alicia's electric bill was $49.22, and her water bill was $22.14. Estimate the total of her utilities for September.

Answer:

Solve the problem by rounding the expenses to the nearest $10.

$49.22 rounds up to $50 because the digit in the ones place is 9.

$22.14 rounds down to $20 because the digit in the ones place is 2.

50 + 20 = 70, so Alicia's September utilities are about **$70**.

Statistics

A **measure of central tendency** is a single value used to describe or represent a set of data. Three common measures of central tendency are mean, median, and mode. A **measure of spread** is a value used to describe the dispersion of data. The simplest measure of spread is range.

A **mean** is an average. The mean is computed by adding all the data and dividing by the number of data points.

The **median** of a set of data is the middle number when the data is ranked (put in order). A data set with an even number of data points will have two numbers in the middle. When that is the case, the median is the mean of those two numbers.

The **range** of a set of data is the difference between the greatest and the least values in the set.

PRACTICE QUESTION

15. Zoe has 6 tests in her chemistry class. Her scores were 75, 62, 78, 92, 83, and 90. What are the mean, median, and range of her test scores?

<u>Answer:</u>

To find the mean, add her scores and divide by 6:

$75 + 62 + 78 + 92 + 83 + 90 = 480$

$\frac{480}{6} = \mathbf{80}$

To find the median, put the scores in order and find the middle term:

From smallest to largest, the data is 62, 75, 78, 83, 90, 92.

The two middle numbers are 78 and 83.

$\frac{78 + 83}{2} = \mathbf{80.5}$

To find the range of Zoe's test scores, subtract the lowest score from the highest score:

$92 - 62 = \mathbf{30}$

Units

The United States uses customary units, sometimes called **standard units.** In this system, there are a number of different units that can be used to describe the same variable. These units and the relationships between them are shown in Table 2.4.

Table 2.4. US Customary Units

Variable Measured	Unit	Conversions
Length	inches, foot, yard, mile	12 inches = 1 foot 3 feet = 1 yard 5,280 feet = 1 mile
Weight	ounces, pound, ton	16 ounces = 1 pound 2,000 pounds = 1 ton
Volume	fluid ounces, cup, pint, quart, gallon	8 fluid ounces = 1 cup 2 cups = 1 pint 2 pints = 1 quart 4 quarts = 1 gallon
Time	second, minute, hour, day	60 seconds = 1 minute 60 minutes = 1 hour 24 hours = 1 day
Area	square inch, square foot, square yard	144 square inches = 1 square foot 9 square feet = 1 square yard

Most other countries use the metric system, which has its own set of units for variables like length, weight, and volume. These units are modified by prefixes that make large and small numbers easier to handle. These units and prefixes are shown in Table 2.5.

Table 2.5. Metric Units and Prefixes

Variable Measured	Base Unit
length	meter
weight	gram
volume	liter

Metric Prefix	Conversion
kilo	base unit × 1,000
hecto	base unit × 100
deka	base unit × 10
deci	base unit × 0.1
centi	base unit × 0.01
milli	base unit × 0.001

 Although the United States uses the customary system, many metric units are commonly used in medical settings, including the kilogram (kg) and milliliter (mL).

Conversion factors are used to convert one unit to another (either within the same system or between different systems). A conversion factor is simply a fraction built from two equivalent values. For example, there are 12 inches in 1 foot, so the conversion factor can be $\frac{12 \text{ in}}{1 \text{ ft}}$ or $\frac{1 \text{ ft}}{12 \text{ in}}$.

To convert from one unit to another, multiple the original value by a conversion factor that has the old and new units.

How many inches are in 6 feet?

$$6 \text{ ft} \times \frac{12 \text{ in}}{1 \text{ ft}} = \frac{6 \text{ ft} \times 12 \text{ in}}{1 \text{ ft}} = 72 \text{ in}$$

PRACTICE QUESTIONS

16. How many centimeters are in 2.5 m?

Answer:
Use a conversion factor to convert centimeters to meters.
$$2.5 \text{ m} \times \frac{100 \text{ cm}}{1 \text{ m}} = \frac{2.5 \text{ m} \times 100 \text{ cm}}{1 \text{ m}} = \textbf{250 cm}$$

17. A newborn baby will consume 4 ounces of milk per meal and eats 6 times a day. If the baby's mother is storing the milk in pints, how many pints will she need in a week?

Answer:
Find the total number of ounces the baby will consume in a week.

4 oz × 6 meals a day × 7 days = 168 oz

Use a conversion factor to convert ounces to pints.
$$168 \text{ oz} \times \frac{1 \text{ cu}}{8 \text{ oz}} \times \frac{1 \text{ pt}}{2 \text{ cu}} = \textbf{10.5 pt}$$

Test Your Knowledge

Work the problem, and then choose the correct answer.

1. $65 - 14.46 + 5.8 =$

   a. 14.53   b. 15.69   c. 44.74   d. 56.34   e. 73.66

2. $4.368 \div 2.8 =$

   a. 0.0156   b. 0.156   c. 1.56   d. 15.6   e. 156

3. Find the product of 0.4 and 0.2.

   a. 0.006   b. 0.06   c. 0.08   d. 0.6   e. 0.8

4. Noah and Jennifer have a total of $10.00 to spend on lunch. If each buys his or her own order of french fries and a soda, how many orders of chicken strips can they share?

Menu	
Item	**Price**
Hamburger	$4.00
Chicken Strips	$4.00
Onion Rings	$3.00
French Fries	$2.00
Soda	$1.00
Shake	$1.00

   a. 0   b. 1   c. 2   d. 3   e. 4

5. A fruit stand sells apples, bananas, and oranges at a ratio of 3:2:1. If the fruit stand sells 20 bananas, how many total pieces of fruit does the fruit stand sell?

   a. 10   b. 30   c. 40   d. 50   e. 60

6. Juan plans to spend 25% of his workday writing a report. If he is at work for 9 hours, how many hours will he spend writing the report?

   a. 2.25   b. 2.50   c. 2.75   d. 3.25   e. 4.00

7. John's rain gauge recorded rain on three consecutive days: $\frac{1}{2}$ in on Sunday, $\frac{2}{3}$ in on Monday, and $\frac{1}{4}$ in on Tuesday. What was the total amount of rain received over the three days?

   a. $\frac{4}{9}$ in   b. $\frac{17}{36}$ in   c. $1\frac{5}{12}$ in   d. $1\frac{1}{2}$ in   e. $1\frac{2}{3}$ in

8. A woman's dinner bill is $48.30. If she adds a 20% tip, what will she pay in total?
    a. $9.66   b. $28.98   c. $38.64   d. $57.96   e. $68.30

9. Frank and Josh need 1 lb of chocolate to bake a cake. If Frank has $\frac{3}{8}$ lb of chocolate, and Josh has $\frac{1}{2}$ lb, how much more chocolate do they need?
    a. $\frac{1}{10}$ lb   b. $\frac{1}{8}$ lb   c. $\frac{3}{5}$ lb   d. $\frac{7}{8}$ lb   e. $\frac{9}{10}$ lb

10. Students in a biology class get the following scores on a test:
    97, 83, 81, 70, 64, 92, 87
    What was the average score?
    a. 64   b. 71   c. 82   d. 92   e. 96

ANSWER KEY

1. d.

Line up the decimals and subtract.

```
  65.00
− 14.46
  50.54
```

Line up the decimals and add.

```
 50.54
+ 5.80
 56.34
```

56.34

2. c.

$4.368 ÷ 2.8 =$ **1.56**

3. c.

$0.4 × 0.2 =$ **0.08**

4. b.

Write an expression to find the number of chicken strips they can afford:

$$\$10 − 2(\$2.00 + \$1.00)$$
$$= \$10 − 2(\$3.00)$$
$$= \$10 − \$6.00 = \$4.00$$

Four dollars is enough money to buy **one order** of chicken strips to share.

5. e.

Assign variables and write the ratios as fractions. Then, cross multiply to solve for the number of apples and oranges sold.

$$\frac{apples}{bananas} = \frac{3}{2} = \frac{x}{20}$$

$$60 = 2x$$

$$x = 30 \text{ apples}$$

$$\frac{oranges}{bananas} = \frac{1}{2} = \frac{y}{20}$$

$$2y = 20$$

$$y = 10 \text{ oranges}$$

To find the total, add the number of apples, oranges, and bananas together.

$30 + 20 + 10 =$ **60 pieces of fruit**

6. a.

Use the equation for percentages.

part = whole × percentage =
$9 × 0.25 =$ **2.25**

7. c.

$$\frac{1}{2} + \frac{2}{3} + \frac{1}{4}$$

$$\frac{6}{12} + \frac{8}{12} + \frac{3}{12} = \frac{17}{12} = 1\frac{5}{12} \text{ in}$$

8. d.

Multiply the total bill by 0.2 (20%) to find the amount of the tip. Then add the tip to the total.

$$\$48.30 × 0.2 = \$9.66$$

$$\$48.30 + \$9.66 = \textbf{\$57.96}$$

9. b.

$$\frac{3}{8} + \frac{1}{2} = \frac{3}{8} + \frac{4}{8} = \frac{7}{8}$$

$$1 − \frac{7}{8} = \frac{8}{8} − \frac{7}{8} = \frac{1}{8} \text{ lb}$$

10. c.

Add the scores and divide by 7:

$$\frac{97 + 83 + 81 + 70 + 64 + 92 + 87}{7} = \frac{574}{7} = \textbf{82}$$

THREE: NONVERBAL SUBTEST

The twenty-five nonverbal questions on the Academic Aptitude test will gauge your spatial visualization and reasoning skills. You will be shown an analogy built from basic shapes, and you will need to select from the five answer choices to complete the analogy.

Nonverbal Question Format

Which shape correctly completes the statement?

○ is to ○ as □ is to ?

a.○ b.□ c.△ d.□ e.◇

What is an Analogy?

An **analogy** presents two sets of words or objects that share a relationship. The relationship is set up using the format

_____ is to _____ as _____ is to _____

Let's start with an example that uses words instead of shapes.

BIRD is to FLOCK as WOLF is to PACK

In this analogy, the first word is an individual animal, and the second word represents a group of those animals. A group of birds is a flock, and a group of wolves is a pack.

Solving analogies requires you to determine the relationship between the first two words, and then use that relationship to fill in the missing word:

SAIL is to BOAT as FLY is to_____

Here, the missing word is *plane*: you sail on a boat and fly on a plane.

Nonverbal Analogies

The nonverbal questions on the test will be in this same format, but they will use shapes instead of words. To answer these questions, you should look for the common relationships between the first two shapes.

ROTATING SHAPES

The first shape is rotated 90 degrees clockwise to give the second shape. To find the missing shape, rotate the cube 90 degrees clockwise as well.

ADDING TO SHAPES

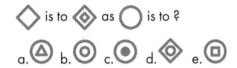

To create the second shape, another diamond is added inside the first. To find the missing shape, add another circle inside the first one.

SUBTRACTING FROM SHAPES

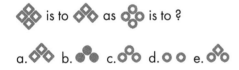

The bottom diamond is removed from the first shape to create the second. To find the missing shape, remove the bottom circle.

COMBINATIONS

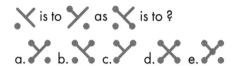

In this question, the first shape is reflected horizontally (as if shown in a mirror). Then, another circle is added to the end of the top line. To find the missing shape, reflect the given shape and add a circle to the end of the top line.

Test Your Knowledge

Which shape correctly completes the statement?

1. ◐ is to ◑ as ⬒ is to ?

   a. ● b. ◑ c. ⬒ d. ◑ e. ○

2. △ is to □ as ⬠ is to ?

   a. ◺ b. ▭ c. ⬡ d. ○ e. ◇

3. | is to ┬ as ┿ is to ?

   a. ⬓ b. ≣ c. ☐ d. ✚ e. ┷

4. ⬠ is to ◇ as ◁ is to ?

   a. △ b. ▭ c. ◸ d. ◀ e. ▽

5. ❖ is to ❖ as ❖ is to ?

   a. ❖ b. ❖ c. ❖ d. ❖ e. ❖

6. ⊪ is to ⊪ as ⊪ is to ?

   a. ▂▃▄ b. ▃▄▅ c. ▅▄▃ d. ▂▃▄ e. ▃▄▅

7. ⊠ is to ⊠ as ⊡ is to ?

   a. ⊠ b. ⊠ c. ⊠ d. ⊡ e. ⊠

8. ⫸ is to ⫷ as ⫶ is to ?

   a. ⫶ b. ⫶ c. ⫶ d. ⫶ e. ⫶

9. ∟ is to | as ⊔ is to ?

   a. ⌐ b. ⌐ c. || d. ▭ e. ⊓

10. ⊏ is to ⊏ as ⊐ is to ?

    a. ⊐ b. ⊏ c. ⊏ d. ⊐ e. ⊏

ANSWER KEY

1. d.

Rotate the first shape 90 degrees clockwise to create the second shape.

2. c.

Add one side to the first shape to create the second shape.

3. d.

Add a horizontal line to the first shape to create the second shape.

4. d.

Cut the first shape in half horizontally to create the second shape.

5. c.

Change the right diamond to a circle in the first shape to create the second shape.

6. b.

Shorten the inside lines of the first shape to create the second shape.

7. b.

The second shape is a horizontal reflection of the first shape.

8. d.

Add a circle to the side that has one circle on the first shape to create the second shape.

9. c.

Remove the bottom bar from the first shape to create the second shape.

10. a.

Reflect the first shape vertically and reverse the shading to create the second shape.

FOUR: SPELLING

The forty-five spelling questions will test your ability to pick out the correct spelling of a word from a list of three choices.

> **Spelling Question Format**
>
> *Each line below contains a word with three different spellings. Select the word from each line that is spelled correctly.*
>
> **1.**   a. intense b. intinse c. entense

As with the verbal questions, a large vocabulary will help you on this section. But when you encounter words you're not familiar with, it will help to know some basic spelling rules. You can also study the list of commonly misspelled words included at the end of this chapter.

Spelling Rule One: Plurals

Regular nouns are made plural by adding *s*. Irregular nouns can follow many different rules for pluralization, which are summarized in Table 4.1.

Table 4.1. Irregular Plural Nouns

Ends with...	Make it plural by...	Example
y	changing *y* to *i* and adding *–es*	baby → babies
f	changing *f* to *v* and adding *–es*	leaf → leaves
fe	changing *f* to *v* and adding *–s*	knife → knives
us	changing *us* to *i*	nucleus → nuclei
ch, o, s, sh, x, z	adding *–es*	catch → catches
		potato → potatoes
		pass → passes
		push → pushes
		annex → annexes
		blitz → blitzes

Table 4.1. Irregular Plural Nouns (continued)

Always the Same	Doesn't Follow the Rules
sheep	man → men
deer	child → children
fish	person → people
moose	tooth → teeth
pants	goose → geese
binoculars	mouse → mice
scissors	ox → oxen

Spelling Rule Two: Conjugating Verbs

The suffixes *–ed* or *–ing* added to a regular verb generally signify the verb's tense. However, there are some exceptions to the general rule for conjugating regular verbs.

When verbs end with a silent *–e*, drop the *e* before adding *–ed* or *–ing*.

fake → faked → faking

ache → ached → aching

When verbs end in the letters *–ee*, do not drop the second *e*. Instead, simply add *–d* or *–ing*.

free → freed → freeing

agree → agreed → agreeing

When the verb ends with a single vowel plus a consonant, and the stress is at the *end* of the word, then the consonant must be doubled before adding *–ed* or *–ing*.

commit → committed → committing

refer → referred → referring

If the stress is not at the end of the word, then the consonant can remain singular.

target → targeted → targeting

visit → visited → visiting

Verbs that end with the letter *–c* must have the letter *k* added before receiving a suffix.

panic → panicked → panicking

Spelling Rule Three: i before e

Generally, the letter *i* comes before the letter *e* in a word except when the *i* is preceded by the letter *c*.

> p<u>ie</u>ce; sal<u>ie</u>nt; c<u>ei</u>ling; con<u>cei</u>vable

There are some notable exceptions where the letter *e* comes before the letter *i* such as:

✦ words that end in –*cien*, like *proficient*
✦ plural words ending in –*cies*, like *policies*
✦ words with an *ay* sound, like *eight*, *vein*, or *neighbor*

 Be cautious of the rule "*i* comes before e except after c" because it has many exceptions. Your foreign neighbors weighed the iciest beige glaciers!

Spelling Rule Four: Suffixes

Change the final –*y* to an *i* when adding a suffix.

> lazy → laziest
>
> tidy → tidily

For words that end with the letters –*le*, replace the letter *e* with the letter *y*.

> subtle → subtly

Commonly Misspelled Words

Table 4.2 shows some commonly misspelled words. It outlines the word as correctly spelled, followed by tips to ensure proper spelling.

Table 4.2. Commonly Misspelled Words

Correct Spelling	Tip
acceptable	has two c's and remember, you are *able* to accept
accommodate, accommodation	double up the c and *m*
acquire, acquit	add a c before *qu*
aggressive, aggression	spelled with two g's
apparently	*ent*, not *ant*

Table 4.2. Commonly Misspelled Words (continued)

Correct Spelling	Tip
appearance	ends with –ance, not –ence
assassination	two sets of double s, like Mississippi
basically	ends with –ally
beginning	add an n before adding the –ing
bizarre	spelled with one z and two r's
calendar	ends with –ar, not –er
colleague	The second half is league, as in baseball; colleagues are like teammates!
completely	do not drop the e; ends with –ely
conscious	spelled with an s and c in the middle
definitely	spelled with ite, not ate
dilemma	double m
disappear	spelled with one s and two p's
disappoint	spelled with one s and two p's
discipline	spelled with an s and c in the middle; i instead of a
embarrass	double up r and s
environment	an n comes before the m
existence	ends with –ence
finally	spelled with two l's
fluorescent	begins with fluor– and ends with –scent
foreign	e before i, an exception to the ie rule
foreseeable	begins with fore–, not for–
forty	begins with for–, not four–
forward	begins with for–, not fo–
further	begins with fur–, not fu–
gist	begins with g, not j
government	there is an n before the m
harass, harassment	spelled with one r, and two s's
idiosyncrasy	ends with –asy, not –acy
incidentally	ends with –ally
independent	ends with –ent, not –ant
interrupt	spelled with two r's
irresistible	ends with –ible

Correct Spelling	Tip
knowledge	remember the silent *d*
liaise, liaison	there is an *i* before and after the *a*: *iai*
necessary	spelled with one *c* and two *s*'s
noticeable	do not drop the *e* when adding *–able*
occasion	spelled with two *c*'s and one *s*
occurred, occurring	spelled with two *c*'s and two *r*'s
occurrence	spelled with two *c*'s and two *r*'s, and ends with *–ence*, not *–ance*
persistent	ends with *–ent*, not *–ant*
possession	two sets of double *s* like *Mississippi*
preferred, preferring	the second *r* is doubled
publicly	simply add *–ly* to the end of *public*
recommend	spelled with two *m*'s
reference	ends with *–ence*, not *–ance*
referred, referring	the second *r* is doubled
relevant	ends with *–ant*, not *–ent*
resistance	ends with *–ance*
sense	ends with *–se*
separate	spelled with *par* in the middle
siege	*i* before *e* rule
successful	double up the *c*'s and *s*'s
supersede	ends with *–sede*
surprise	begins with *sur–*, not *su–*
tendency	ends with *–ency*, not *–ancy*
tomorrow	spelled with one *m* and two *r*'s
tongue	begins with *ton–* and ends with *–gue*
unforeseen	spelled with an *e* after the *r*
unfortunately	do not drop the *e* when adding *–ly*
until	spelled with one *l* at the end
weird	*e* before *i*, an exception to the rule

Test Your Knowledge

Each line below contains a word with three different spellings. Select the word from each line that is spelled correctly.

1. a. supervise   b. supervice   c. supirvise
2. a. casuelty   b. casualty   c. cacualtie
3. a. intensity   b. entensity   c. intensitie
4. a. acelerate   b. accelarate   c. accelerate
5. a. permenent   b. permanent   c. permanant
6. a. abundent   b. abbundant   c. abundant
7. a. burdan   b. burden   c. bourden
8. a. prioritys   b. priorities   c. prioretees
9. a. immense   b. emmense   c. emmence
10. a. contaminate   b. contamenate   c. conntaminate
11. a. arterys   b. arteries   c. artarys
12. a. nutrishon   b. nutrition   c. nutretion
13. a. accomplesh   b. acommplish   c. accomplish
14. a. comppasion   b. compassion   c. commpasion
15. a. courteous   b. corteous   c. curtaous

ANSWER KEY

1. a.
2. b.
3. a.
4. c.
5. b.
6. c.
7. b.
8. b.
9. a.
10. a.
11. b.
12. b.
13. c.
14. b.
15. a.

FIVE: READING

The thirty-five reading questions will test your ability to understand the purpose, structure, and key ideas of written passages. The test will present short passages, often on a scientific topic, that are followed by a set of questions with four answer choices.

Reading Question Format

Read each passage carefully. Each question is followed by four suggested answers. You are to decide which one of these answers you should choose based upon the material in the passage.

In 1953, doctors surgically removed the hippocampus of patient Henry Molaison in an attempt to stop his frequent seizures. Unexpectedly, he lost the ability to form new memories, leading to the biggest breakthrough in the science of memory. Molaison's long-term memory—of events more than a year before his surgery—was unchanged as was his ability to learn physical skills.

1.   After surgery to remove his hippocampus, Henry Molaison no longer

a. formed new memories b. had seizures c. learned physical skills
d. remembered his past

The Main Idea

The **topic** is a word or short phrase that explains what a passage is about. The **main idea** is a complete sentence that explains what the author is trying to say about the topic. Generally, the **topic sentence** is the first (or near the first) sentence in a paragraph. It is a general statement that introduces the topic so that the reader knows what to expect.

? To find the main idea, identify the topic and then ask, *What is the author trying to tell me about the topic?*

The **summary sentence**, on the other hand, frequently (but not always!) comes at the end of a paragraph or passage because it wraps up all the ideas presented. This sentence summarizes what an author has said about the topic. Some passages, particularly short ones, will not include a summary sentence.

Table 5.1. Identifying Topic and Main Idea	
The cisco, a foot-long freshwater fish native to the Great Lakes, once thrived throughout the basin but had virtually disappeared by the 1950s. However, today fishermen are pulling them up by the net load in Lake Michigan and Lake Ontario. It is highly unusual for a native species to revive, and the reason for the cisco's reemergence is even more unlikely. The cisco have an invasive species—quagga mussels—to thank for their return. Quagga mussels depleted nutrients in the lakes, harming other species highly dependent on these nutrients. Cisco, however, thrive in low-nutrient environments. As other species—many of which were invasive—diminished, cisco flourished in their place.	
topic sentence	The cisco, a foot-long freshwater fish native to the Great Lakes, once thrived throughout the basin but had virtually disappeared by the 1950s.
topic	cisco
summary sentence	As other species—many of which were invasive—diminished, cisco flourished in their place.
main idea	Cisco had nearly disappeared from the lake but now flourish thanks to the invasive quagga mussels.

PRACTICE QUESTIONS

1. Tourists flock to Yellowstone National Park each year to view the geysers that bubble and erupt throughout it. What most of these tourists do not know is that these geysers are formed by a caldera—a hot crater in the earth's crust—which was created by a series of three eruptions of an ancient super volcano. These eruptions, which began 2.1 million years ago, spewed between 1,000 and 2,450 cubic kilometers of volcanic matter at such a rate that the volcano's magma chamber collapsed, creating the craters.

   The paragraph above is chiefly concerned with

   a. tourists
   b. geysers
   c. volcanic eruptions
   d. super volcanos

   Answer:

   b. is correct. The topic of the passage is geysers. Tourists, volcanic eruptions, and super volcanos are all mentioned in the explanation of what geysers are and how they are formed.

2. The Battle of Little Bighorn, commonly called Custer's Last Stand, was a battle between the Lakota, the Northern Cheyenne, the Arapaho, and the Seventh Cavalry Regiment of the US Army. Led by war leaders Crazy Horse and Chief Gall and the religious leader Sitting Bull, the allied tribes of the Plains Indians decisively defeated their US foes. Two hundred and sixty-eight US soldiers were killed, including General George Armstrong Custer, two of his brothers, his nephew, his brother-in-law, and six Indian scouts.

The main idea of the passage is that

a.   most of General Custer's family died in the Battle of Little Bighorn

b.   the Seventh Cavalry regiment was formed to fight Native American tribes

c.   Sitting Bull and George Custer were fierce enemies

d.   the Battle of Little Bighorn was a significant victory for the Plains Indians

<u>Answer:</u>

d. is correct. The author writes that "the allied tribes...decisively defeated their US foes," and the remainder of the passage provides details to support this idea.

Supporting Details

Statements that describe or explain the main idea are **supporting details**. Supporting details are often found after the topic sentence. They support the main idea through examples, descriptions, and explanations.

 To find supporting details, look for sentences that connect to the main idea and tell more about it.

Authors may add details to support their argument or claim. **Facts** are details that point to truths, while **opinions** are based on personal beliefs or judgments. To differentiate between fact and opinion, look for statements that express feelings, attitudes, or beliefs that can't be proven (opinions) and statements that can be proven (facts).

Table 5.2. Supporting Details and Fact and Opinion	
Bait is an important element of fishing. Some people use live bait, such as worms and night crawlers. Others use artificial bait, such as lures and spinners. Live bait has a scent that fish are drawn to. Live bait is a good choice for fishing. It's cheap and easy to find. Lures can vibrate, make noise, and mimic the movements of some fish. People should choose artificial bait over live bait because it can be used multiple times.	
supporting details	Lures can vibrate, make noise, and mimic the movements of some fish.
fact	Live bait has a scent that fish are drawn to.
opinion	Live bait is a good choice for fishing.

PRACTICE QUESTIONS

The greatest changes in sensory, motor, and perceptual development happen in the first two years of life. When babies are first born, most of their senses operate in a similar way to those of adults. For example, babies are able to hear before they are born; studies show that babies turn toward the sound of their mothers' voices just minutes after being born, indicating they recognize the mother's voice from their time in the womb.

The exception to this rule is vision. A baby's vision changes significantly in his or her first year of life; initially babies have a range of vision of only 8 – 12 inches and no depth perception. As a result, infants rely primarily on hearing; vision does not become the dominant sense until around the age of 12 months.

3. To perceive the world, babies primarily rely on

a. vision b. hearing c. touch d. smell

Answer:

b. is correct. The passage states that "infants rely primarily on hearing."

4. In the first year of life, a baby has no

a. depth perception b. vision c. hearing d. motor skills

Answer:

a. is correct. The passage states that "[a] baby's vision changes significantly in its first year of life; initially babies have a range of vision of only 8 – 12 inches and no depth perception."

Drawing Conclusions

Readers can use information that is **explicit**, or clearly stated, along with information that is **implicit**, or indirect, to make inferences and **draw conclusions**. Readers can determine meaning from what is implied by using details, context clues, and prior knowledge. When answering questions, consider what is known from personal experiences and make note of all information the author has provided before drawing a conclusion.

 Look for facts, character actions and dialogue, how each sentence connects to the topic, and the author's reasoning for an argument when drawing conclusions.

Table 5.3. Drawing Conclusions

When the Spanish-American War broke out in 1898, the US Army was small and understaffed. President William McKinley called for 1,250 volunteers to serve in the First US Volunteer Cavalry. The ranks were quickly filled by cowboys, gold prospectors, hunters, gamblers, Native Americans, veterans, police officers, and college students looking for an adventure. The officer corps was composed of veterans of previous wars. With more volunteers than it could accept, the army set high standards: all the recruits had to be skilled on horseback and with guns. Consequently, they became known as the Rough Riders.

question	Why are the volunteers named Rough Riders?
explicit information	different people volunteered, men were looking for adventure, recruits had to be extremely skilled on horseback and with guns due to a glut of volunteers

implicit information	Men had previous occupations; officer corps veterans worked with volunteers.
conclusion drawn	The men were called Rough Riders because they were inexperienced yet particularly enthusiastic to help with the war and were willing to put in extra effort to join.

PRACTICE QUESTION

5. Alfie closed his eyes and took several deep breaths. He was trying to ignore the sounds of the crowd, but even he had to admit it was hard not to notice the tension in the stadium. He could feel 50,000 sets of eyes burning through his skin—this crowd expected perfection from him. He took another breath and opened his eyes, setting his sights on the soccer ball resting peacefully in the grass. One shot, just one last shot, between his team and the championship. He didn't look up at the goalie, who was jumping nervously on the goal line just a few yards away. Afterward, Alfie would swear he didn't remember anything between the referee's whistle and the thunderous roar of the crowd.

At the end of the passage, it's most likely that Alfie

a. passed out on the field and was unable to take the shot

b. had his shot blocked by the goalie

c. scored the goal and won his team the championship

d. was too scared to take the shot

<u>Answer:</u>

c. is correct. The crowd's support for Alfie and their collective roar after the shot imply that Alfie scored the goal and won the championship.

The Author's Purpose and Point of View

The **author's purpose** is an author's reason for writing a text. Authors may write to share an experience, entertain, persuade, or inform readers. This can be done through persuasive, expository, and narrative writing.

Persuasive writing influences the actions and thoughts of readers. Authors state an opinion, and then provide reasons that support the opinion. **Expository writing** outlines and explains steps in a process. Authors focus on a sequence of events. **Narrative writing** tells a story. Authors include a setting, plot, characters, problem, and solution in the text.

 Use the acronym **PIES**—*persuade, inform, entertain, state*—to help you remember elements of an author's purpose.

Authors also share their **point of view** (perspectives, attitudes, and beliefs) with readers. Readers can identify the author's point of view by word choice, details, descriptions, and characters' actions. The author's attitude or **tone** can be found in word choice that conveys feelings or stance on a topic.

Text structure is the way the author organizes a text. A text can be organized to show problem and solution, comparison and contrast, or even cause and effect. Structure of a text can give insight into an author's purpose and point of view. If a text is organized to pose an argument or advertise a product, it can be considered persuasive. The author's point of view will be revealed in how thoughts and opinions are expressed in the text.

Table 5.4. The Author's Purpose and Point of View	
Superfoods are foods found in nature. They contain rich nutrients and are low in calories. Many people are concerned about healthy diets and weight loss, so superfoods are a great meal choice! Rich antioxidants and vitamins found in superfoods decrease the risk of diseases and aid in heart health.	
author's purpose	persuade readers of the benefit of superfoods
point of view	advocate superfoods as "a great meal choice"
tone	positive, encouraging, pointing out the benefits of superfoods, using positive words like *great* and *rich*
structure	cause and effect to show use of superfoods and results

PRACTICE QUESTIONS

6.   University of California, Berkeley, researchers decided to tackle an age-old problem: why shoelaces come untied. They recorded the shoelaces of a volunteer walking on a treadmill by attaching devices to record the acceleration, or g-force, experienced by the knot. The results were surprising. A shoelace knot experiences more g-force from a person walking than any rollercoaster can generate. However, if the person simply stomped or swung his or her feet—the two movements that make up a walker's stride—the g-force was not enough to undo the knots.

The purpose of the passage is to

a.   confirm if shoelaces always come undone

b.   compare the force of treadmills and rollercoasters

c.   persuade readers to tie their shoes tighter

d.   describe the results of an experiment on shoelaces

Answer:

d. is correct. The text provides details on the experiment as well as its results.

7. What do you do with plastic bottles? Do you throw them away, or do you recycle or reuse them? As landfills continue to fill up, there will eventually be no place to put our trash. If you recycle or reuse bottles, you will help reduce waste and turn something old into a creative masterpiece!

The author of the passage believes that

a. landfills are unnecessary

b. reusing objects requires creativity

c. recycling helps the environment

d. reusing objects is better than recycling

<u>Answer:</u>

c. is correct. The author states that recycling and reusing objects reduce waste, which helps the environment.

8. Negative cinematic representations of gorillas have provoked fear and contribute to hunting practices that endanger gorilla populations. It's a shame that many films portray them as scary and aggressive creatures. Their size and features should not be cause for alarm. Gorillas are actually shy and act aggressively only when provoked.

The main emotion expressed by the author toward gorillas is

a. surprise b. concern c. anger d. fear

<u>Answer:</u>

b. is correct. The author is concerned that the scary depiction of gorillas in cinema is harming public perceptions of the animal.

Test Your Knowledge

Read each passage carefully. Each question is followed by four suggested answers. You are to decide which one of these answers you should choose based upon the material in the passage.

The cisco, a foot-long freshwater fish native to the Great Lakes, once thrived throughout the basin but had virtually disappeared by the 1950s. However, today fishermen are pulling them up by the net load in Lake Michigan and Lake Ontario. It is highly unusual for a native species to revive, and the reason for the cisco's reemergence is even more unlikely. The cisco have an invasive species—quagga mussels—to thank for their return. Quagga mussels depleted nutrients in the lakes, harming other species highly dependent on these nutrients. Cisco, however, thrive in low-nutrient environments. While quagga mussels caused the death of many other native species, cisco flourished in their place.

1. The cisco population has grown in recent years because of

    a.   quagga mussels

    b.   fishing

    c.   a high-nutrient environment

    d.   the availability of more food

2. In the Great Lakes, quagga mussels have

    a.   died out due to overfishing

    b.   been the main source of food for cisco

    c.   struggled to survive in their new environments

    d.   caused the decline of native species

When a fire destroyed San Francisco's American Indian Center in October of 1969, American Indian groups set their sights on the recently closed island prison of Alcatraz as the site of a new Indian cultural center and school. Ignored by the government, an activist group known as Indians of All Tribes sailed to Alcatraz in the early morning hours with eighty-nine men, women, and children. They landed on Alcatraz, claiming it for all the tribes of North America. Their demands were ignored, and so the group continued to occupy the island for the next nineteen months, its numbers swelling up to 600 as others joined. By January of 1970, many of the original protestors had left, and on June 11, 1971, federal marshals forcibly removed the last residents.

3. In October 1969, Alcatraz was occupied by

    a.   San Francisco's American Indian Center

    b.   Indians of All Tribes

    c.   federal marshals

    d.   prisoners

For thirteen years, a spacecraft called *Cassini* was on an exploratory mission to Saturn. The spacecraft was designed not to return but to end its journey by diving into Saturn's atmosphere. This dramatic ending provided scientists with unprecedented information about Saturn's atmosphere and its magnetic and gravitational fields. First, however, *Cassini* passed Saturn's largest moon, Titan, where it recorded data on Titan's curious methane lakes, gathering information about potential seasons on the planet-sized moon. Then it passed through the unexplored region between Saturn itself and its famous rings. Scientists hope to learn how old the rings are and to directly examine the particles that make them up. *Cassini's* mission ended in 2017, but researchers have new questions for future exploration.

4. The scientists who developed *Cassini* want to learn more about Titan's

    a.   gravity
    b.   rings
    c.   lakes
    d.   atmosphere

In a remote nature preserve in northeastern Siberia, scientists are attempting to re-create the subarctic grassland ecosystem that flourished there during the last Ice Age. The area today is dominated by forests, but the lead scientists of the project believe the forested terrain was not a natural development. They believe that if they can restore the grassland, they will be able to slow climate change by slowing the thawing of the permafrost that lies beneath the surface. Key to this undertaking is restoring the wildlife to the region, including wild horses, musk oxen, bison, and yak. Most ambitiously, the scientists hope to revive the woolly mammoth species, which was key in trampling the ground and knocking down the trees, helping to keep the land free for grasses to grow.

5. Today, northeastern Siberia is dominated by

    a.   forests
    b.   grasslands
    c.   wild horses
    d.   woolly mammoths

The heart works by shifting between two states: systole and diastole. In systole, the cardiac muscles are contracting and moving blood from any given chamber. During diastole, the muscles are relaxing and the chamber is expanding to fill with blood. The systole and diastole are responsible for blood pressure—the pressure in the major arteries. This is the blood pressure that is measured in a regular exam. The two values are systolic and diastolic pressures, respectively. Because it is measured when blood is being pumped into the arteries, systolic blood pressure is always the higher number.

Systolic blood pressure is correlated with negative health outcomes such as stroke and heart failure. For this reason, doctors categorize patients based on their systolic blood pressure. These categories are given in the following table.

Categories	Systolic Range
normal	< 120
prehypertension	120 – 139
hypertension stage 1	140 – 159
hypertension stage 2	160 – 179
hypertensive crisis	> 180

6. A person with a blood pressure of 151/95 be categorized as

   a.   normal

   b.   prehypertension

   c.   hypertension stage 1

   d.   hypertension stage 2

The social and political discourse of America continues to be permeated with idealism. An idealistic viewpoint asserts that the ideals of freedom, equality, justice, and human dignity are the truths that Americans must continue to aspire to. Idealists argue that truth is what should be, not necessarily what is. In general, they work to improve things and to make them as close to ideal as possible.

7. The purpose of the passage is to

   a.   advocate for freedom, equality, justice, and human rights

   b.   explain what an idealist believes in

   c.   explain what's wrong with social and political discourse in America

   d.   persuade readers to believe in certain truths

Alexander Hamilton and James Madison called for the Constitutional Convention to write a constitution as the foundation of a stronger federal government. Madison and other Federalists like John Adams believed in separation of powers, republicanism, and a strong federal government. Despite the separation of powers that would be provided for in the US Constitution, anti-Federalists like Thomas Jefferson called for even more limitations on the power of the federal government.

8. A strong federal government was NOT supported by

   a.   Alexander Hamilton

   b.   James Madison

   c.   John Adams

   d.   Thomas Jefferson

After looking at five houses, Robert and I have decided to buy the one on Forest Road. The first two homes we visited didn't have the space we need—the first had only one bathroom, and the second did not have a guest bedroom. The third house, on Pine Street, had enough space inside but didn't have a big enough yard for our three dogs. The fourth house we looked at, on Rice Avenue, was stunning but well above our price range. The last home, on Forest Road, wasn't in the neighborhood we wanted to live in. However, it had the right amount of space for the right price.

9. The house on Pine Street
   a. did not have enough bedrooms
   b. did not have a big enough yard
   c. was not in the right neighborhood
   d. was too expensive

The study showed that private tutoring is providing a significant advantage to those students who are able to afford it. Researchers looked at the grades of students who had received free tutoring through the school versus those whose parents had paid for private tutors. The study included 2,500 students in three high schools across four grade levels. The study found that students who used private tutoring increased their grade point average (GPA) by 0.7 points. Students who used the school's free tutor service saw an increase in GPA of 0.3 points on average. Students who used both services showed an increase in GPA of 0.5 points. After reviewing the study, the board is recommending that the school restructure its free tutor service to provide a more equitable education for all students.

10. The students with the largest rise in GPA used
    a. no tutoring
    b. free tutoring
    c. private tutoring
    d. free and private tutoring

It could be said that the great battle between the North and South we call the Civil War was a battle for individual identity. The states of the South had their own culture, one based on farming, independence, and the rights of both man and state to determine their own paths. Similarly, the North had forged its own identity as a center of centralized commerce and manufacturing. This clash of lifestyles was bound to create tension, and this tension was bound to lead to war. But people who try to sell you this narrative are wrong. The Civil War was not a battle of cultural identities—it was a battle about slavery. All other explanations for the war are either a direct consequence of the South's desire for wealth at the expense of her fellow man or a fanciful invention to cover up this sad portion of our nation's history. And it cannot be denied that this time in our past was very sad indeed.

11. The purpose of the passage is to
    a. convince readers that slavery was the main cause of the Civil War
    b. illustrate the cultural differences between the North and the South before the Civil War
    c. persuade readers that the North deserved to win the Civil War
    d. demonstrate that the history of the Civil War is too complicated to be understood clearly

12. Before the Civil War, the North had a culture based on

    a.   farming

    b.   independence

    c.   rights of the state

    d.   centralized commerce

The bacteria, fungi, insects, plants, and animals that live together in a habitat have evolved to share a pool of limited resources. They've competed for water, minerals, nutrients, sunlight, and space—sometimes for thousands or even millions of years. As these communities have evolved, the species in them have developed complex, long-term interspecies interactions known as symbiotic relationships.

Ecologists characterize these interactions based on whether each party benefits. In mutualism, both individuals benefit, while in synnecrosis, both organisms are harmed. A relationship where one individual benefits and the other is harmed is known as parasitism. Examples of these relationships can easily be seen in any ecosystem. Pollination, for example, is mutualistic—pollinators get nutrients from the flower, and the plant is able to reproduce—whereas tapeworms, which steal nutrients from their host, are parasitic.

There's yet another class of symbiosis that is <u>controversial</u> among scientists. As it's long been defined, commensalism is a relationship where one species benefits and the other is unaffected. But is it possible for two species to interact and for one to remain completely unaffected? Often, relationships described as commensal include one species that feeds on another species' leftovers; remoras, for instance, will attach themselves to sharks and eat the food particles they leave behind. It might seem like the shark gets nothing from the relationship, but a closer look will show that sharks in fact benefit from remoras, which clean the sharks' skin and remove parasites. In fact, many scientists claim that relationships currently described as commensal are just mutualistic or parasitic in ways that haven't been discovered yet.

13. In the last paragraph, the word *controversial* means

    a.   debatable

    b.   disbelieved

    c.   confusing

    d.   upsetting

14. The relationship between a tapeworm and its host is

    a.   mutualism

    b.   commensalism

    c.   parasitism

    d.   synnecrosis

15. The purpose of the passage is to

    a.   argue that commensalism isn't actually found in nature

    b.   describe the many types of symbiotic relationships

    c.   explain how competition for resources results in long-term interspecies relationships

    d.   provide examples of the many different ways individual organisms interact

ANSWER KEY

1. a.

The passage explains how quagga mussels depleted the nutrients in the lake, allowing cisco to thrive.

2. d.

The author writes that the "quagga mussels caused the death of many other native species."

3. b.

The "Indians of All Tribes sailed to Alcatraz" because they wanted to develop a cultural center and school at the site.

4. c.

The author writes that the *Cassini* "recorded data on Titan's curious methane lakes."

5. a.

The passage states that "[t]he area today is dominated by forests."

6. c.

A systolic blood pressure reading of 151 (the higher number) places the patient in the hypertension stage 1 category.

7. b.

The purpose of the passage is to explain what an idealist believes in. The author does not offer any opinions or try to persuade readers about the importance of certain values.

8. d.

In the passage, Thomas Jefferson is defined as an anti-Federalist, in contrast with Federalists who believed in a strong federal government.

9. b.

The author says that the house on Pine Street "had enough space inside but didn't have a big enough yard for [their] three dogs."

10. c.

Students who used private tutoring services increased their GPA by 0.7 points, which is more than the free tutoring service (0.3) or a combination of the two (0.5).

11. a.

The author writes, "But people who try to sell you this narrative are wrong. The Civil War was not a battle of cultural identities—it was a battle about slavery."

12. d.

The passage states that "the North had forged its own identity as a center of centralized commerce."

13. a.

The author writes that "[t]here's yet another class of symbiosis that is controversial among scientists" and goes on to say that "many scientists claim the relationships currently described as commensal are just mutualistic or parasitic in ways that haven't been discovered yet." This implies that scientists debate about the topic of commensalism.

14. b.

The author writes that "[a]s these communities have evolved, the species in them have developed complex, long-term interspecies interactions known as symbiotic relationships." She then goes on to describe the different types of symbiotic relationships that exist.

15. c.

The author writes that "tapeworms, which steal nutrients from their host, are parasitic."

SIX: LIFE SCIENCE

Biological Molecules

Molecules that contain carbon bound to hydrogen are **organic molecules**. Large organic molecules that contain many atoms and repeating units are **macromolecules**. Many macromolecules are **polymers** composed of repeating small units called **monomers**. There are four basic biological macromolecules that are common between all organisms: carbohydrates, lipids, proteins, and nucleic acids.

Carbohydrates, also called sugars, are polymers made of carbon, hydrogen, and oxygen atoms. The monomer for carbohydrates are **monosaccharides**, such as glucose and fructose, that combine to form more complex sugars called **polysaccharides**. Carbohydrates store energy and provide support to cellular structures.

Lipids, commonly known as fats, are composed mainly of hydrogen and carbon. They serve a number of functions depending on their particular structure: they make up the membrane of cells and can act as fuel, as steroids, and as hormones. Lipids are hydrophobic, meaning they repel water.

Proteins serve an incredibly wide variety of purposes within the body. As enzymes, they play key roles in important processes like DNA replication, cellular division, and cellular metabolism. Structural proteins provide rigidity to cartilage, hair, nails, and the cytoskeletons (the network of molecules that holds the parts of a cell in place). They are also involved in communication between cells and in the transportation of molecules.

 An **enzyme** is a protein that accelerates a specific chemical reaction.

Proteins are composed of individual **amino acids**, which are joined together by peptide bonds to form **polypeptides**. There are twenty amino acids, and the order of the amino acids in the polypeptide determines the shape and function of the molecule.

Nucleic acids store hereditary information and are composed of monomers called **nucleotides**. Each nucleotide includes a sugar, a phosphate group, and a nitrogenous base.

There are two types of nucleic acids. **Deoxyribonucleic acid (DNA)** contains the genetic instructions to produce proteins. It is composed of two strings of nucleotides wound into a double helix shape. The "backbone" of the helix is made from the nucleotide's sugar (deoxyribose) and phosphate groups. The "rungs" of the ladder are made from one of four nitrogenous bases: adenine, thymine, cytosine, and guanine. These bases bond together in specific pairs: adenine with thymine and cytosine with guanine.

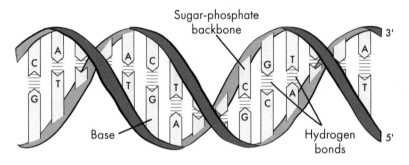

Figure 6.1. The Structure of DNA

Ribonucleic acid (RNA) transcribes information from DNA and plays several vital roles in the replication of DNA and the manufacturing of proteins. RNA nucleotides contain a sugar (ribose), a phosphate group, and one of four nitrogenous bases: adenine, uracil, cytosine, and guanine. It is usually found as a single-stranded molecule. There are three main differences between DNA and RNA:

1. DNA contains the nucleotide thymine; RNA contains the nucleotide uracil.
2. DNA is double-stranded; RNA is single-stranded.
3. DNA is made from the sugar deoxyribose; RNA is made from the sugar ribose.

PRACTICE QUESTIONS

1. The monomers that make up proteins are called
    a. monosaccharides
    b. nucleotides
    c. amino acids
    d. polypeptides
    e. enzymes

    Answer:

    c. is correct. Amino acid monomers are the building blocks of proteins.

2. Nucleic acids' primary purpose is to store
    a. carbon
    b. proteins
    c. water
    d. chemical energy
    e. genetic information

Nucleic Acids

DNA stores information by coding for proteins using blocks of three nucleotides called **codons**. Each codon codes for a specific amino acid; together, all the codons needed to make a specific protein are called a **gene**. In addition to codons for specific amino acids, there are also codons that signal "start" and "stop."

The production of a protein starts with **transcription**. During transcription, the two sides of the DNA helix unwind and a complementary strand of messenger RNA (mRNA) is manufactured using the DNA as a template.

This mRNA then travels outside the nucleus where it is "read" by a ribosome during **translation**. Each codon on the mRNA is matched to an anti-codon on a strand of tRNA, which carries a specific amino acid. The amino acids bond as they are lined up next to each other, forming a polypeptide.

When it is not being transcribed, DNA is tightly wound around proteins called **histones** to create **nucleosomes**, which are in turn packaged into **chromatin**. The structure of chromatin allows large amounts of DNA to be stored in a very small space and helps regulate transcription by controlling access to specific sections of DNA. Tightly folding the DNA also helps

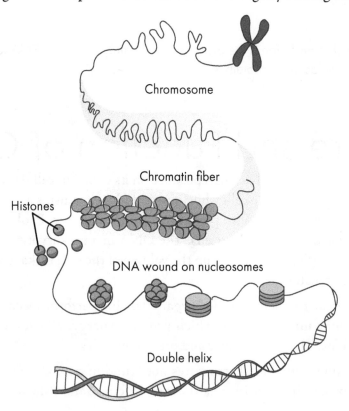

Figure 6.2. DNA, Chromatin, and Chromosomes

prevent damage to the genetic code. Chromatin is further bundled into packages of DNA called **chromosomes**. During cell division, DNA is replicated to create two identical copies of each chromosome called **chromatids**.

Somatic (body) cells are **diploid**, meaning they carry two copies of each chromosome—one inherited from each parent. Gametes, which are reproductive cells, are **haploid** and carry only one copy of each chromosome. Human somatic cells have forty-six chromosomes, while human egg and sperm each carry twenty-three chromosomes.

A **mutation** causes a change in the sequence of nucleotides within DNA. For example, the codon GAC codes for the amino acid aspartic acid. However, if the cytosine is swapped for adenine, the codon now reads GAA, which corresponds to the amino acid glutamic acid. Germ-line mutations, or mutations that occur in a cell that will become a gamete, can be passed on to the offspring of an organism. Somatic mutations cannot be passed on to the offspring of an organism.

PRACTICE QUESTION

3. The information stored in RNA is used to produce a protein during

  a. replication

  b. translation

  c. transcription

  d. photosynthesis

  e. respiration

Answer:

b. is correct. Translation is the process of matching codons in RNA to the correct anti-codon to manufacture a protein.

Structure and Function of Cells

A **cell** is the smallest unit of life that can reproduce on its own. Unicellular organisms, such as amoebae, are made up of only one cell, while multicellular organisms are comprised of many cells. There are two basic types of cells: prokaryotic and eukaryotic. **Prokaryotic cells**, which include most bacteria, do not have a nucleus. The DNA in a prokaryotic cell is carried in the **cytoplasm**, which is the fluid that makes up the volume of the cell. **Eukaryotic cells** contain a nucleus where genetic material is stored.

Cells contain smaller structures called **organelles** that perform specific functions within the cell. These include **mitochondria**, which produce energy; **ribosomes**, which produce proteins; and **vacuoles**, which store water and other molecules.

Plant cells include a number of structures not found in animal cells. These include the **cell wall**, which provides the cell with a hard outer structure, and **chloroplasts**, where photosynthesis occurs.

The outer surface of human cells is made up of a **plasma membrane**, which gives the cell its shape. This membrane is primarily composed of a **phospholipid bilayer**, which itself is made up of two layers of lipids that face opposing directions. This functions to separate the inner cellular environment from the extracellular space, the space between cells. Molecules travel through the cell membrane using a number of different methods:

+ **Diffusion** occurs when molecules pass through the membrane from areas of high to low concentration.

+ **Facilitated diffusion** occurs with the assistance of proteins embedded in the membrane.

+ **Osmosis** is the movement of water from areas of high to low concentration.

+ During **active transport**, proteins in the membrane use energy (in the form of ATP) to move molecules across the membrane.

PRACTICE QUESTION

4.   The structure that stores genetic material in a cell is the

a.   nucleus

b.   chloroplast

c.   ribosome

d.   vacuole

e.   mitochondrion

Answer:

a. is correct. Genetic material (DNA) is stored in the nucleus.

Cellular Respiration

Organisms use chains of chemical reactions called **biochemical pathways** to acquire, store, and use energy. The molecule most commonly used to store energy is **adenosine triphosphate (ATP)**. When a phosphate group (Pi) is removed from ATP, creating **adenosine diphosphate (ADP)**, energy is released. The cell harnesses this energy to perform processes such as transport, growth, and replication.

Cells also transfer energy using the molecules **nicotinamide adenine dinucleotide phosphate (NADPH)** and **nicotinamide adenine dinucleotide (NADH)**. These molecules are generally used to carry energy-rich electrons during the process of creating ATP.

In **cellular respiration**, food molecules such as glucose are broken down, and the electrons harvested from these molecules are used to make ATP. The first stage of cellular respiration is an **anaerobic** (does not require oxygen) process called **glycolysis**. Glycolysis takes place in the cytoplasm of a cell and transforms glucose into two molecules of pyruvate. In the process, two molecules of ATP and two molecules of NADH are produced.

Under anaerobic conditions, pyruvate is reduced to acids and sometimes gases and/or alcohols in a process called **fermentation.** However, this process is less efficient than aerobic cellular respiration and produces only two ATP.

Under aerobic conditions, pyruvate enters the second stage of cellular respiration—the **Krebs cycle.** The Krebs cycle takes place in the mitochondria, or tubular organelles, of a eukaryotic cell. Here, pyruvate is oxidized completely to form six molecules of carbon dioxide (CO_2). This set of reactions also produces two more molecules of ATP, ten molecules of NADH, and two molecules of $FADH_2$ (an electron carrier).

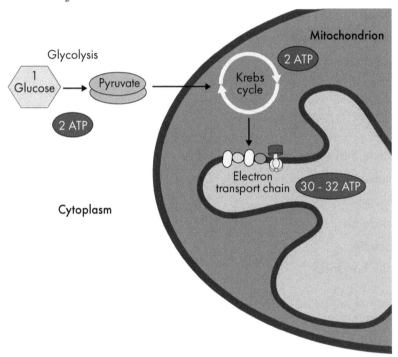

Figure 6.3. Cellular Respiration

The electrons carried by NADH and $FADH_2$ are transferred to the **electron transport chain,** where they cascade through carrier molecules embedded in the inner mitochondrial membrane. Oxygen is the final electron receptor in the chain; it reacts with these electrons and hydrogen to form water. This sequential movement of electrons drives the formation of a proton (H^+) gradient, which is used by the enzyme ATP synthase to produce ATP. The electron transport chain produces thirty to thirty-two molecules of ATP.

The balanced chemical equation for cellular respiration is:

$$C_6H_{12}O_6 + 6O_2 \rightarrow 6CO_2 + 6H_2O$$

5. The stage of cellular respiration that produces the largest number of ATP molecules is

    a. glycolysis
    b. fermentation
    c. the Krebs cycle
    d. the electron transport chain
    e. the citric acid cycle

    Answer:

    d. is correct. The electron transport chain produces thirty to thirty-two molecules of ATP made during cellular respiration. The other choices each produce only two molecules of ATP.

Photosynthesis

The sun powers nearly all biological systems on this planet. Plants, along with some bacteria and algae, harness the energy of sunlight and transform it into chemical energy through the process of **photosynthesis.**

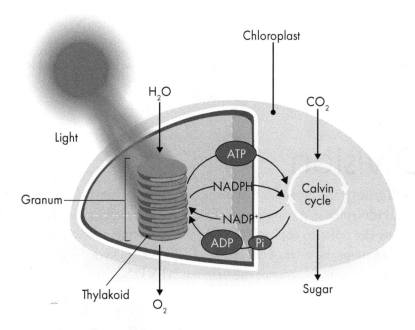

Figure 6.4. Photosynthesis

Inside each chloroplast are stacks of flat, interconnected sacs called **thylakoids**. Within the membrane of each thylakoid sac are light-absorbing pigments called **chlorophyll**.

In the light-dependent reactions of photosynthesis, light penetrates the chloroplast and strikes the chlorophyll. The energy in the sunlight excites electrons, boosting them to a higher energy level. These excited electrons then cascade through the **electron transport chain**, creating energy in the form of ATP and NADPH. This reaction also splits water to release O_2.

The ATP and NADPH created by the light-dependent stage of photosynthesis enter the **Calvin cycle**, which uses the energy to produce the carbohydrate glucose $(C_6H_{12}O_6)$. The carbon needed for this reaction comes from atmospheric CO_2.

The balanced chemical equation for photosynthesis is:

$$6CO_2 + 6H_2O \rightarrow C_6H_{12}O_6 + 6O_2$$

PRACTICE QUESTION

6. Glucose is produced during the Calvin cycle using

    a. O_2

    b. CO_2

    c.   ADP

    d. H_2

    e. N_2

Answer:

b. is correct. During the Calvin cycle, carbon dioxide (CO_2) is used to produce glucose.

Cell Division

The process of cell growth and reproduction is the **cell cycle**. Eukaryotic cells spend the majority of their lifespan in **interphase**, during which the cell performs necessary functions and grows. During interphase, the cell also copies its DNA. Then, during **mitosis** the two identical sets of DNA are pulled to opposite sides of the cell. The cell then splits during **cytokinesis**, resulting in two cells that have identical copies of the original cell's DNA.

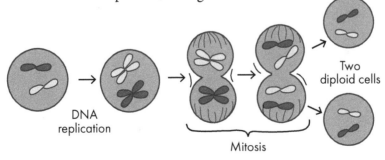

Figure 6.5. Mitosis

Meiosis is the process of sexual reproduction, or the formation of gametes (egg and sperm cells). During meiosis, the replicated DNA is separated to form two diploid cells. These cells in turn will separate again, with each cell retaining a single set of chromosomes. The result is four haploid cells.

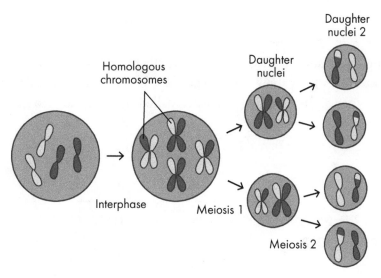

Figure 6.6. Meiosis

PRACTICE QUESTION

7. The result of mitosis and cytokinesis is

   a. two haploid cells

   b. four haploid cells

   c. eight haploid cells

   d. two diploid cells

   e. four diploid cells

   Answer:

   d. is correct. The daughter cells produced during mitosis are genetically identical to their diploid (2n) parent.

Genetics

Genetics is the study of heredity—how characteristics are passed from parents to offspring. These characteristics, or traits, are determined by genes. Each individual has two versions of the same gene, called **alleles**, with one contributed by each parent. An individual is **homozygous** for a particular gene if both alleles are the same, and **heterozygous** if the two alleles are different.

 Alleles are written as a single letter with the dominant allele capitalized (A) and the recessive allele lowercase (a).

For a particular gene, the **dominant** allele will always be expressed, and the **recessive** allele will only be expressed if the other allele is also recessive. In other words, a recessive trait is only expressed if the individual is homozygous for that allele.

The full set of genetic material in an organism is its **genotype**. The organism's **phenotype** is the set of observable traits in the organism. For example, brown hair is a phenotype. The genotype of this trait is a set of alleles that contain the genetic information for brown hair.

The genotype, and resulting phenotype, of sexually reproducing organisms can be tracked using **Punnett squares**, which show the alleles of the parent generation on each of two axes. The possible genotypes of the resulting offspring, called the F1 generation, are then shown in the body of the square.

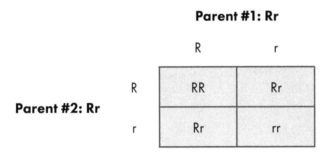

Figure 6.7. Punnett Square

In Figure 6.8., two heterozygous parents for trait R are mated, resulting in the following genotypes and phenotypes for the offspring:

+ 1 homozygous dominant (dominant phenotype)
+ 2 heterozygous (dominant phenotype)
+ 1 homozygous recessive (recessive phenotype)

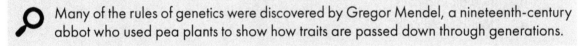

Many of the rules of genetics were discovered by Gregor Mendel, a nineteenth-century abbot who used pea plants to show how traits are passed down through generations.

Non-Mendelian inheritance describes patterns that do not follow the ratios described above. These patterns can occur for a number of reasons. Alleles might show **incomplete dominance**, where one allele is not fully expressed over the other, resulting in a third phenotype (for example, a red flower and white flower cross to create a pink flower). Alleles can also be **codominant**, meaning both are fully expressed (such as the AB blood type).

The expression of genes can also be regulated by mechanisms other than the dominant/recessive relationship. For example, some genes may inhibit the expression of other genes, a process called **epistasis**. The environment can also impact gene expression. For example, organisms with the same genotype may grow to different sizes depending on the nutrients available to them.

8. The dominant allele will not be expressed when

    a. a recessive allele from the father is paired with a recessive allele from the mother

    b. a dominant allele from the father is paired with a dominant allele from the mother

    c. a dominant allele from the father is paired with a recessive allele from the mother

    d. a recessive allele from the father is paired with a dominant allele from the mother

    e. a recessive allele from the father is paired with no allele from the mother

Answer:

a. is correct. This genotype is homozygous, and the recessive trait is the only trait that can be expressed.

9. Alleles for brown eyes (B) are dominant over alleles for blue eyes (b). If two parents are both heterozygous for this gene, the percent chance that their offspring will have brown eyes is

    a. 0 percent

    b. 25 percent

    c. 50 percent

    d. 75 percent

    e. 100 percent

Answer:

d. is correct. The Punnett square shows that there is a 75 percent chance the child will have the dominant B gene, and thus have brown eyes.

	B	**b**
B	BB	Bb
b	Bb	bb

Evolution

Evolution is the gradual genetic change in species over time. Natural selection alters the variation and frequency of certain alleles and phenotypes within a population. This increased variation and frequency leads to varying reproductive success, in which individuals with certain traits survive over others. Combined, these mechanisms lead to gradual changes in the genotype of individual populations that, over time, can result in the creation of a new species.

Natural selection is a process in which only the members of a population best adapted to their environment tend to survive and reproduce, which ensures that their favorable traits will be passed on to future generations of the species. There are four basic conditions that must be met in order for natural selection to occur:

1. inherited variation
2. overproduction of offspring
3. fitness to environment
4. differential reproduction

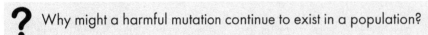 Why might a harmful mutation continue to exist in a population?

The offspring with inherited variations best suited for their environment will be more likely to survive than others and are therefore more likely to pass on their successful genes to future populations through reproduction. This is referred to as **fitness**. An organism that is considered biologically "fit" will be more successful passing on its genes through reproduction compared to other members of the population. The frequency of certain alleles in a gene pool will change as a result.

Artificial selection occurs in a species when humans get involved in the reproductive process. Over time, humans have intentionally bred organisms with the same desirable traits in a process called selective breeding. This has led to the evolution of many common crops and farm animals that are bred specifically for human consumption, as well as among domesticated animals, such as horses or dogs.

PRACTICE QUESTION

10. Natural selection is NOT occurring when
   a. peahens select the most brightly colored peacocks as mates
   b. large bears chase smaller rivals away from food sources
   c. sparrows with a certain beak shape reach plentiful food sources
   d. farmers plant seeds only from the most productive corn plants
   e. male ibex use their horns to fight other males before mating with females

   Answer:
   d. is correct. Farmers choosing specific traits in plants is an example of artificial selection.

Ecology

Ecology is the study of organisms' interactions with each other and the environment. Ecologists break down the groups of organisms and abiotic features into hierarchal groups.

Groups of organisms of the same species living in the same geographic area are called **populations**. These organisms will compete with each other for resources and mates and will display characteristic patterns in growth related to their interactions with the environment. For example, many populations exhibit a carrying capacity, which is the highest number of individuals that the resources in a given environment can support. Populations that outgrow their carrying capacity are likely to experience increased death rates until the population reaches a stable level again.

Populations of different species living together in the same geographic region are called **communities**. Within a community there are many different interactions among individuals of different species. **Predators** consume **prey** for food, and some species are in **competition** for the same limited pool of resources. In a **symbiotic** relationship, two species have evolved to share a close relationship. Two species may also have a **parasitic** relationship in which one organism benefits to the detriment of the other, such as ticks feeding off a dog. Both species benefit in a **mutualistic** relationship, and in a **commensalistic** relationship, one species benefits and the other feels the effects.

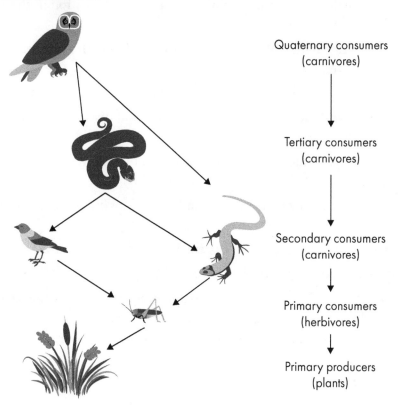

Figure 6.8. Food Web

Within a community, a species exists in a **food web**: every species either consumes or is consumed by another (or others). The lowest trophic level in the web is occupied by **producers**, which include plants and algae that produce energy directly from the sun. The next level are **primary consumers** (herbivores), which consume plant matter. The next trophic level includes **secondary consumers** (carnivores), which consume herbivores.

Answer:

b. is correct. Precipitation is a nonliving (abiotic) factor that influences population size.

12. The terrestrial biome characterized by moderate rainfall and the dominance of deciduous trees is called
   a. desert
   b. tropical rainforest
   c. temperate forest
   d. tundra
   e. grasslands

Answer:

c. is corret. Temperate forests have moderate rainfall and are dominated by deciduous trees.

Human Anatomy and Physiology

In a multicellular organism, cells are grouped together into **tissues**, and these tissues are grouped into **organs**, which perform specific **functions**. The heart, for example, is the organ that pumps blood throughout the body. Organs are further grouped into **organ systems**, such as the digestive or respiratory systems.

Anatomy is the study of the structure of organisms, and **physiology** is the study of how these structures function. Both disciplines study the systems that allow organisms to perform a number of crucial functions, including the exchange of energy, nutrients, and waste products with the environment. This exchange allows organisms to maintain **homeostasis**, or the stabilization of internal conditions.

> In science, a **system** is a collection of interconnected parts that make up a complex whole with defined boundaries. Systems may be closed, meaning nothing passes in or out of them, or open, meaning they have inputs and outputs.

The human body has a number of systems that perform vital functions, including the digestive, excretory, respiratory, circulatory, skeletal, muscular, immune, nervous, endocrine, and reproductive systems.

The **digestive system** breaks food down into nutrients for use by the body's cells. Food enters through the **mouth** and moves through the **esophagus** to the **stomach**, where it is physically and chemically broken down. The food particles then move into the **small intestine**, where the majority of nutrients are absorbed. Finally, the remaining particles enter the **large intestine**, which mostly absorbs water, and waste exits through the **rectum** and **anus**. This system also includes other organs, such as the **liver**, **gallbladder**, and **pancreas**, that manufacture substances needed for digestion.

The **genitourinary system** removes waste products from the body. Its organs include the liver, which breaks down harmful substances, and the **kidneys**, which filter waste from the bloodstream. The excretory system also includes the **bladder** and **urinary tract**, which expel the waste filtered by the kidneys; the lungs, which expel the carbon dioxide created by cellular metabolism; and the skin, which secretes salt in the form of perspiration.

The **respiratory system** takes in oxygen (which is needed for cellular functioning) and expels carbon dioxide. Humans take in air primarily through the nose but also through the mouth. This air travels down the **trachea** and **bronchi** into the **lungs**, which are composed of millions of small structures called alveoli that allow for the exchange of gases between the blood and the air.

The circulatory system carries oxygen, nutrients, and waste products in the blood to and from all the cells of the body. The

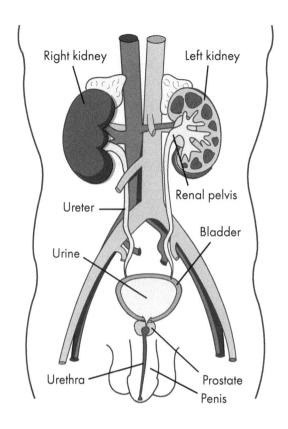

Figure 6.9. Genitourinary System

heart is a four-chambered muscle that pumps blood throughout the body. The four chambers are the right atrium, right ventricle, left atrium, and left ventricle. Deoxygenated blood (blood

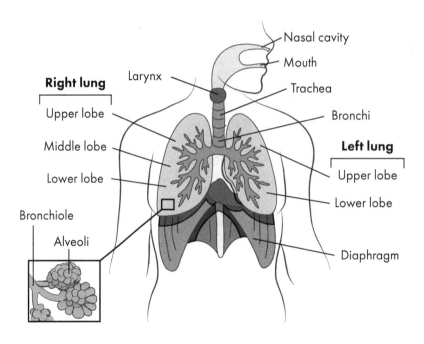

Figure 6.10. Respiratory System

from which all the oxygen has been extracted and used) enters the right atrium and then is sent from the right ventricle through the pulmonary artery to the lungs, where it collects oxygen. The oxygen-rich blood then returns to the left atrium of the heart and is pumped out the left ventricle to the rest of the body.

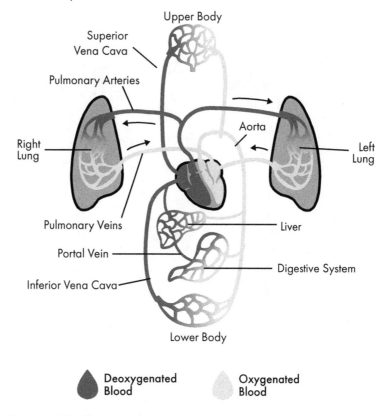

Figure 6.11. Circulatory System

Blood travels through a system of vessels. **Arteries** branch directly off the heart and carry blood away from it. The largest artery is the aorta, which carries blood from the heart to the rest of the body. **Veins** carry blood back to the heart from other parts of the body. Most veins carry deoxygenated blood, but the pulmonary veins carry oxygenated blood from the lungs back to the heart to then be pumped to the rest of the body. Arteries and veins branch into smaller and smaller vessels until they become **capillaries**, which are the smallest vessels and the site where gas exchange occurs.

The **skeletal system**, which is composed of the body's **bones** and **joints**, provides support for the body and helps with movement. Bones also store some of the body's nutrients and produce specific types of cells. Humans are born with 237 bones. However, many of these bones fuse during childhood, and adults have only 206 bones. Bones can have a rough or smooth texture and come in four basic shapes: long, flat, short, and irregular.

The **muscular system** allows the body to move and also moves blood and other substances through the body. The human body has three types of muscles. Skeletal muscles are voluntary muscles (meaning they can be controlled) that are attached to bones and move the body. Smooth muscles are involuntary muscles (meaning they cannot be controlled) that create movement in parts of the digestive tract, blood vessels, and the reproduction system. Finally, cardiac muscle is the involuntary muscle that contracts the heart, pumping blood throughout the body.

> Some skeletal muscles, such as the diaphragm and those that control blinking, can be voluntarily controlled but usually operate involuntarily.

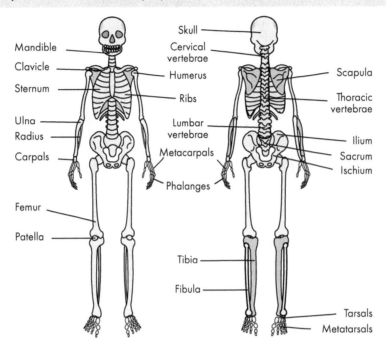

Figure 6.12. The Skeletal System

The **immune system** protects the body from infection by foreign particles and organisms. It includes the **skin** and mucous membranes, which act as physical barriers, and a number of specialized cells that destroy foreign substances in the body. The human body has an adaptive immune system, meaning it can recognize and respond to foreign substances once it has been exposed to them. This is the underlying mechanism behind vaccines.

The immune system is composed of **B cells**, or B lymphocytes, that produce special proteins called **antibodies** that bind to foreign substances, called **antigens**, and neutralize them. **T cells**, or T lymphocytes, remove body cells that have been infected by foreign invaders like bacteria or viruses. **Helper T cells** coordinate production of antibodies by B cells and removal of infected cells by T cells. **Killer T cells** destroy body cells that have been infected by invaders after they are identified and removed by T cells. Finally, **memory cells** remember antigens that have been removed so the immune system can respond more quickly if they enter the body again.

> Memory B cells are the underlying mechanisms behind vaccines, which introduce a harmless version of a pathogen into the body to activate the body's adaptive immune response.

The **nervous system** processes external stimuli and sends signals throughout the body. It is made up of two parts. The central nervous system (CNS) includes the brain and spinal cord and is where information is processed and stored. The brain has three parts: the cerebrum,